PLEASE DON'T PUSH MY BUTTONS

THE BIBLE'S RESPONSE TO OUR ANGRY WORLD

REVEREND ROBERT SELEKMAN

SILVERSMITH
P R E S S

Published by Silversmith Press–Houston, Texas
www.silversmithpress.com

Please Don't Push My Buttons

First Edition
Copyright © 2024 Robert Selekman

The views and opinions expressed herein belong to the author
and do not necessarily represent those of the publisher.

ISBN 978-1-961093-44-7 (Softcover Book)
ISBN 978-1-961093-45-4 (eBook)

This book is dedicated to Colonel Tim Tatum, US Army, Chaplain Corps, Retired. Over many decades, Tim has always been there for me. First as one of my Seminary Professors, then as my Senior Chaplain while an Intern, and later as an ongoing mentor and friend when I became a Police Chaplain and Ordained Minister. While transitioning from full-time work to the next phase of my life of volunteering, I sought his godly advice, and he recommended that I be more like Abram (Abraham), step out in faith, and get on my camel. Well, I did that and ended up overseas doing missionary work. I eventually returned to the US, staying in touch with Tim and continuing to serve the local church and community.

CONTENTS

Section Three
The Anger Solution

Section Four
Now What?

PREFACE

As a twenty-year-old college student, I worked in construction during the summer. One day, around mid-morning, I found breathing difficult due to the stagnant air. To make matters worse, one of my coworkers made fun of me in front of a half dozen other workers.

This coworker was a bully. He was more vocal than others and seemed to enjoy being cruel, especially in front of a crowd. But on this day, I didn't feel much like being made fun of, and I was certainly in no mood for a confrontation. So I asked him nicely to stop making fun of me. But this day was different and possibly more dangerous because I held a long-handled pick.

As I gripped the tool ever tighter, I felt that if this bully was going to make one more stinging and hurtful comment, I might have to shut him up permanently! I was just about ready to blow my stack and physically fight back. Because if you take your adversary out, you get rid of the problem, right?

And then it happened. I became enraged and saw red. I mean, I literally saw red, and it scared me! But something inside of me said: "STOP!" Heeding the warning, I knew I needed to leave immediately! I had to go home and cool off. So I turned around, found my boss, and told him I needed to leave or would have it out with this guy. Fortunately, my boss agreed with me. I then got in my car, went home, and cooled off. In the following days, I avoided this bully. Eventually, I started back to school and never saw this person again. But I think his behavior probably continued (and likely caught up with him).

And me? I learned I needed to identify the "hot buttons" that could make me mad. If I ever saw red again or got close to it, I needed to get out of the situation as soon as possible.

So, do you ever get angry? Is your temper under control, or do you often lack self-control? Do you tend to get mad over little things or big things? Do you hold a grudge? Have you ever said or done something wrong in a heated argument, or do you walk away from a confrontation? Have you ever reached the boiling point where it might lead to hatred, bitterness, or unforgiveness? Most importantly, have you ever sat down and identified those buttons you don't want to be pushed?

This book is intended to help you identify those hot buttons and, if pushed, how to act accordingly.

Therefore, consider it a journey learning more about yourself, striving to be a loving person, and treating others as you would want to be treated while living in a seemingly unforgiving, angry, and self-centered world.

Will you or I ever stop being angry? The answer is perhaps yes and perhaps no. In our humanness, it is less likely. But with God's grace, the Holy Spirit, and God's Word, change is conceivable: ". . . all things are possible with God" (Mark 10:27 NIV).

Because God treats us with love and forgiveness, we should treat others likewise:

> *Therefore, as God's chosen people, holy and dearly loved, clothe yourselves with compassion, kindness, humility, gentleness and patience. Bear with each other and forgive one another if any of you has a grievance against someone. Forgive as the Lord forgave you. And over all these virtues put on love, which binds them all together in perfect unity.* (Colossians 3:12–14 NIV)

ACKNOWLEDGEMENTS

I am grateful to Gray Pennell and Tony Paige for their encouraging words while reading the initial draft. A special thank you to Pat Rios for the countless proof-reading hours and the many comments and suggestions offered. A much-deserved thanks to Rebekah McKamie for the many recommendations and professional editing to complete this work. And the sincerest appreciation to Joanna Hunt and Silversmith Press for making the manuscript available for print.

ANGRY PEOPLE IN AN ANGRY WORLD

CHAPTER 1

ARE YOU AN
ANGRY PERSON?

If possible, so far as it depends on you,
be at peace with all people.

(Romans 12:18 NASB)

Why do we get so angry sometimes and at other times not so much? Would you take your anger out on your teacher, boss, or a police officer? Probably not, because the consequences could be severe, such as getting kicked out of school, fired, or possibly arrested; none make for a good day or positive outcome.

What about a perfect stranger who might provoke you? Or those closest to us—a neighbor, a coworker, or even a loved one who might anger you? Would you lash out, claim your right to defend yourself, and verbally fight back, knowing the consequences may not be as drastic? Or would you respond by turning the other cheek, saying a kind word, or just walking away?

How, then, are we to respond when placed in an uncomfortable situation? If we respond solely based on our humanness in the here and now, our response will be self-directed and self-centered. However, if we are aware of a spiritual aspect with a blessed future of eternal life, we might respond in ways that are others-directed and others-centered.

In the heat of battle, do we consider these three key aspects of being a Christian?

1. Our citizenship in heaven (Philippians 3:20)
2. Our ministry of reconciliation (2 Corinthians 5:18)
3. Being ambassadors for Christ (2 Corinthians 5:20)

Clearly, then, if we know certain things might trigger us, shouldn't we first try to understand *why* they make us angry? It might be just as important to figure out *who* we are and what makes us tick to resolve any anger issues.

Let's begin by taking a subjective three-part assessment on anger and anger management. Since anger is an emotion, it is a behavior that can be seen and also felt. Within this introspective self-assessment, we will be addressing proneness to anger, how you view (act toward) others, and if you are at the tipping point. The answers can be: never, seldom, frequently, or always.

Proneness to anger
1. Do you need help with self-control?
2. Are you apt to lose your temper?
3. Are you a touchy, sensitive person?
4. Are you easily offended?
5. Is it difficult for you to take criticism?
6. Are you impatient (waiting in line, in traffic, on the phone, etc.)?
7. Are you quick to respond when in a confrontation?
8. Has anyone ever told you that you have anger issues?

How you view others
1. Are you critical of others?
2. Do you judge others?
3. Do you have a hard time forgiving others?
4. Do you keep a record of wrongs (hold a grudge)?
5. Is it hard for you to apologize?
6. Are you a controller?
7. Are you self-seeking?
8. Are you overly serious?
9. Are you an aggressive person?

At the tipping point
1. Do you feel like giving someone a piece of your mind?
2. Is there a situation that makes you mad?
3. Is there something you dislike to do?
4. Is there an issue you hate to talk about?

5. Is there someone you can't stop saying unkind words about?
6. Is there someone you refuse to see?
7. Have you ever sought payback?
8. Have you ever seen red?

If you have answered never/seldom to most of the questions, you appear to exercise self-control and are less likely to get angry. Suppose you have answered frequently/always to most of the questions, especially if you are at the tipping point. In that case, this book can help identify hot buttons, any anger issues, and also provide possible remedies not previously explored.

This next set of questions is how you see yourself and treat others with all pretenses removed. The answers can be: never, seldom, frequently, or always.

How you view yourself
1. Do you feel you are a likable person?
2. Do you consider responses other than getting angry?
3. Do you like yourself?
4. Do you have a sense of humor?
5. Do you recognize others' feelings when in a confrontational situation?
6. Do you love others?
7. Are you at peace with yourself? Others? The world?
8. Are you others-centered?

9. Do you have a relationship with God?
10. Have you ever called Bible verses to mind when confronted by an angry person?
11. Have you ever prayed for others?

If you have answered frequently/always to most of the questions, you already have a good grasp of who you are. You understand anger, how to respond appropriately to those who are angry, and you are less likely yourself to get angry. If you have responded never/ seldom to most of the questions, then this book may help to improve on those Christian traits and behaviors where they might be lacking.

The answers above, followed by the subsequent chapters, will help us better understand what can cause anger in our lives. Armed with that knowledge, we will be in the best position, especially in adverse situations, to do the godly and right thing to live at peace with all.

CHAPTER 2

OUR HOT BUTTONS

In chapter one, you were asked if you tend to have any anger issues. This chapter will look at possible hot buttons and test you when placed in varying (hot button) scenarios.

So how does one identify a hot button? First, think about situations, issues, things, etc., that have gotten you irritated or annoyed. Those are possible buttons. They become hot buttons if, when pushed, you become angry, lose control, or feel another emotion. Second, what was your response? Think about what happened and what you did. Were there possibly other viable options?

Further, ask yourself if this was a Christian response. If not, possibly seek guidance from godly folks, search the Bible for instructive verses, pray, and read on. Finally, because our hot buttons might change based on factors such as age, being aware of this will help us better identify new hot buttons and respond accordingly.

Let's begin. Perhaps you've been in these situations yourself or you know someone else who has. When we might be apt to lose our temper, what do we think, how do we feel, how do we act, and what do we say?

These scenarios address a broad spectrum of what one might expect going through life. They include a cross section of circumstances such as being threatened, disrespected, avoided, betrayed, bullied, and falsely accused. Perhaps what follows might even be an ongoing situation in your life that you might want to address today to prevent things from getting worse in the future.

Indeed, it is prudent to recognize when we are at the advent of an angry moment. We can then calm down, exercise self-control, and avoid a confrontation. In humbleness, we can serve others and consider their interests, showing kindness and consideration of their feelings.

> *Do nothing from selfishness or empty conceit, but with humility of mind regard one another as more important than yourselves; do not merely look out for your own personal interests, but also for the interests of others.* (Philippians 2:3–4 NASB)

Anger is among many other emotions we possess and *can* be controlled. If anger is *not* controlled, it can lead to arguments, physical and emotional abuse, bitterness, rage, physical violence, and long-term health issues, among many other negative results. That is certainly not what any of us as Christians want of ourselves or for others.

Because we are all different, we also will respond differently. The Bible has many verses that can advise us in responding to certain situations or things that might anger us. It follows that it is not enough to recognize *what* makes us angry but also *how* we respond.

While not all-inclusive, the following is a good sampling of situations that one may face and possible responses. Of course, there are many other possible answers, so you might want to review each question again and see how you would respond, if other than those provided. But for now, I ask that you choose one of the three.

Again, the key takeaway in this chapter is to recognize what might push our buttons and what options are available when they are pushed. I ask that you respond truthfully; therefore, select what you *would* do and not what you *should* do.

How would you respond when . . . ?

1) Threatened. You are driving your car in the middle of three lanes. The car ahead of you is going too slow. You signal and then change lanes to the left in front of a truck, believing there is enough room. The truck driver doesn't think so, speeds up, passes you on the right side, and then appears to yell at you. *What do you do?*

    a) Pray quickly, wave nicely, and safely get away from the other driver.
    b) Avoid eye contact and safely get away from the other driver.
    c) Get angry, roll down your window, yell something not so nice, and possibly engage in road rage.

2) Disrespected. You are at the store, and you have now finished shopping. You're happy you have all your items, and now you are headed to the checkout line. As you stand in line, leaving a lane for others to pass in front of you, you are surprised when another person cuts in line with their cart full of their items. They act as if you are not there. *What do you do?*

    a) Pray, smile, and let it go.
    b) Ask the person politely if they saw you or not.
    c) Get angry and tell the person off for disrespecting you.

3) Avoided. You have finally put some savings away, and you are doubly blessed because God has provided for all your needs. But then a close friend asks to borrow some money from you. You go ahead and lend them the needed money. They tell you they will pay you back, but they never do. They make all efforts to avoid you. *What do you do?*

a) Pray for understanding, forgive the debt, and make it a gift.
b) Confront them and tell them you didn't appreciate how the whole situation unfolded and attempt to set up a repayment plan.
c) Get angry and break off the relationship.

4) Betrayed. You are speaking to a very close confidant, and you have told them a very painful and personal story about a mutual acquaintance. You ask them to please not tell anyone else. Two weeks later, you are with this confidant and joined with two other friends at lunch. As the meal begins, the close confidant then blurts out critical parts of the personal story and then asks you to explain yourself. *What do you do?*

a) Pray for strength, say no thanks, and change the topic immediately.
b) Look at the person with surprise and expound on the story.
c) Get angry and tell the person off for betraying you.

5) Bullied. You are talking to several people in the office when the boss shows up. The boss singles you out and starts to yell at you, though they are not specific with any details. They then turn around and storm out in a huff. Your coworkers look at you with extreme pity because the boss is usually very nice.

You know you are in trouble because you must have done something very, very wrong to earn a reprimand. But you are clueless about what you've done. *What do you do?*

    a) Pray for the boss and let it go.
    b) Do not see the boss under any circumstances, believing they might blow up again.
    c) Get angry, see the boss, and tell them off.

6) Brushed aside. In this age of smartphones, it is often more comfortable to send a text message instead of initiating or returning a call. You make a call this time because you want some clarification from an individual. After attempting to call the person over ten times, and several weeks later, you continue to receive a text reply: "I can't talk right now." They still do not return your calls. *What do you do?*

    a) Pray for them and be understanding that they might be swamped.
    b) Leave a voice and text message saying that you are exasperated and very disappointed in them.
    c) Get angry and break off the relationship.

7) Let go. You seek another position within the same company because you are tired of your current workload. You go to your boss and ask to be moved to another position. The following month, you have reassigned responsibilities, believing they are looking for another job for you. You get an email to meet with your boss with the subject line stating: "The way ahead." Excited that a possible new position will be discussed, you attend the meeting. You notice your boss is not alone; a human resources representative is seated with him. You know something is up. Asked to sit down, your boss immediately says, "You are being laid off," and they then follow up with a, "But it's not personal." *What do you do?*

   a) Pray, accept the fact that God is in control and that they are just doing their jobs.
   b) In shock, you cannot believe what is going on and shut down to what is being said.
   c) Get angry and tell the boss that they betrayed you.

8) Falsely accused. You have just moved into your new home, and you notice a scratch on the dining room table that wasn't there before. You call the moving company owner, and they send a craftsman out to look at it. The craftsman shows up and looks at the scratch on top of the table and says, "I can't fix that." You ask, "Why not?" They say, "Because you damaged the table, not the movers." *What do you do?*

   a) Pray and calmly ask the person to explain their comments.
   b) Deny the accusation and defend yourself.
   c) Get angry and throw the person out of your home.

9) Ignored. You are waiting in line, with two cashiers assisting other customers. One cashier is waiting on a couple, but there appears to be some issue taking time. Another cashier is just finishing up, and you're glad to be next. You happen to look around at the store, and when you turn around, that second cashier is gone. You wait another four to five minutes and then call out to the first cashier (still helping the couple), "Can I get some help, please?" That cashier looks at you with what looks like an annoyed face. However, they ask for help to come. At this point, four more people are behind you, all waiting on the disappearing cashier. Still, no one shows up and time keeps passing by. *What do you do?*

   a) Pray, and when finally attended to, ask the cashier why it is taking so long.
   b) When eventually helped, tell the cashier you are annoyed and ask to speak to the manager.
   c) Get angry and say out loud: "You lost a customer," and then walk out in a huff.

10) Broken up. Almost all of us have been through a painful breakup, and unfortunately, it might have ended up in a heated exchange. Months before, the person you are in love with has abruptly ended the close relationship and wants to be "just" friends. You try to accommodate them, yet your heartstrings are being pulled, and it's getting to be too painful. You have realized you can't go on this way, especially since they found someone else. Later, they call you while that someone else is out of town, and you are asked to meet for coffee. You say no. The conversation gets heated, and the person calls you a jerk. *What do you do?*

    a) Pray, hold your tongue, and let the conversation end.
    b) Become hurt and start arguing with the person.
    c) Get angry and hang up.

If most of your answers are (a), you are prone to leading a godly life and caring for and loving others. If most of your answers are (b), you might consider improving your Christian walk and giving God a more significant role in your life. If any of your answers are (c), you could be distant or creating distance from God. By learning to be closer to God, trusting Him and giving Him control in all circumstances, you will then have the ability to respond more constructively rather than angrily.

Regardless of your answers, whether anger is an isolated or frequent occurrence, all can benefit from this book because of the many biblical insights for spiritual growth, inner peace, and practical applications dealing with self-control and anger issues. And if you are wondering where these scenarios came from, well, they all happened to me. I confess my answers were not always an (a). However, I learned from each scenario and made improvements to my life as needed; identifying my buttons helped a lot. If they moved into a hot button situation, I would pray, be patient, put others first, empathize, and use other supporting actions mentioned in the book. As you read on, keep in mind the things you would like to try. In doing so, I pray you find what works best for you to love and live at peace with all.

CHAPTER 3

WHY DO WE GET SO MAD?

What is the first thing that comes to your mind when you think of anger? As you read the following anger idioms, reflect on how they make you feel, especially if you have encountered folks (or possibly you as well) leading to the expression of the anger emotion.

Lose your cool, blow your top, blow your stack, see red, flip out, go bananas, jump up and down, go ballistic, fit to be tied, go postal, have a cow, go off the deep end, fly off the handle, bent out of shape, blow up, lose your temper, throw a temper tantrum, go nuclear, have a hissy fit, blow a gasket, reach the boiling point, have a conniption, go nuts, go crazy, have had enough, ticked off, and so on.

These words probably don't make you feel too good. Anger rarely engenders positive, kind, or helpful thoughts resulting in desirable behavior—it frequently does the opposite. If not addressed and controlled, anger can end up being hurtful to others, as well as to oneself. Fortunately, such harm can be prevented.

These Points to Ponder lay the biblical groundwork for Christian living in an angry world.

1. **Anger starts with a thought.**
   Emotions invariably begin with a thought or an idea. Simply put, if one can control thoughts of or about anger, one can control anger itself. This is key to anger management. What we are thinking about will often result in follow-on behavior. To be sure, how we think is how we go.

   > *For as he thinketh in his heart, so is he.* (Proverbs 23:7 KJV)

2. **Angry thoughts can be captured.**
   One of the most powerful tools one can use is to capture thoughts or ideas. We can consciously give them over to God to handle as they come into our minds. We need not dwell on them or let them get out of control, especially when these thoughts may lead to anger. Ergo, this is one of the best ways to prevent angry behavior.

   > *Casting down imaginations, and every high thing that exalteth itself against the knowledge of God, and bringing into captivity every*

thought to the obedience of Christ. (2 Corinthians 10:5 KJV)

3. **As Christians, we are called to control our anger.**
Keeping our tempers in check will slow us to become angry, and in doing so, we will be less likely to sin. We need to practice behaviors that promote self-control, discipline, and patience.

> *This you know, my beloved brethren. But everyone must be quick to hear, slow to speak and slow to anger; for the anger of man does not achieve the righteousness of God.* (James 1:19–20 NASB)

4. **Anger is less likely to occur if our eyes are focused on God.**
We will be more apt to do godly things and act accordingly if we think about spiritual things. If not, we can be hampered or distracted by many earthly things, keeping our eyes down here and taking our eyes off God.

> *Set your minds on the things above, not on the things that are on earth.* (Colossians 3:2 NASB)

5. **Anger can cloud one's judgment.**
Anger affects our emotional state, often changing our mental state of mind. This can create a battle inside, where unclear and irrational thinking

becomes "rational." With judgment clouded, wrong decisions are made. One might believe they are trying to do the "right" thing when they are actually doing something wrong—i.e., Moses killing an Egyptian (Exodus 2:12), Paul persecuting and killing Christians (Acts 8:3), etc.

> *Refrain from anger and turn from wrath; do not fret—it leads only to evil.* (Psalm 37:8 NIV)

6. **There are many reasons for being angry.**
Though there are many reasons for human anger in the Bible, four primary reasons stand out—unforgiveness, hatred, revenge, and sin. Because of our human and sinful nature, the need to seek personal justice can often be at the forefront of one's mind. It frequently starts as an annoyance, then continues as an irritation, whether from the same source or a cumulation of unaddressed hassles. This irritation can now grow and fester just as a wound would. If not treated, it might reach the tipping point, often resulting in anger, hatred, uncontrolled jealousy, bitterness, rage, etc. And unfortunately, the result may be aggression and violence. Therefore, this is how we should act:

> *Get rid of all bitterness, rage and anger, brawling, and slander, along with every form of malice.* (Ephesians 4:31 NIV)

7. **God's anger is not the same as our (human) anger.**

Above all else, God's anger is righteous, just, and holy. It is often described as wrathful; however, it is not out of spite. God's wrath comes from a verdict meted out for human evil, disobedience, or a sinful act. Here are some notable examples of this:

- God destroyed Sodom and Gomorrah because of immorality (Genesis 19:1–29).
- God flooded the world, and all humanity perished save eight because of immorality (Genesis 6–7).
- God delivered ten plagues in Egypt and then destroyed their army because of Pharaoh's hardened heart (Exodus 7–11, 14:4-28).
- God allowed Israel to be conquered and taken away by the Assyrians because of disobedience and idol worshipping (2 Kings 17:1–23).

If a human gets angry, it is best to leave wrath and vengeance in God's hands.

> Do not take revenge, my dear friends, but leave room for God's wrath, for it is written: "It is mine to avenge; I will repay," says the Lord. (Romans 12:19 NIV)

8. **Anger has consequences.**

When we are angry, do any of us ask what will happen next? In other words, if you or I become mad and no longer capable of clear-headed thinking, with our judgment clouded, how can we even consider what the result will be? I've noticed a recurring theme in the Bible, whereby anger completely overwhelms a person and then dominates their subsequent actions. Many of them could not (or would not) calm down enough to seek other alternatives to their situation.

We are not so different from those in the Bible. Sometimes *we* too might choose wrongly and end up on a less-than-desirable path, not considering how it might affect our future. Cain was in this category. He ended up banished because of his wrong choices and probably never saw his parents again. God further placed a mark upon him. It was a reminder till the end of his days for what he had become—a wrongdoer and murderer who chose not to control his anger (Genesis 4:8–15).

Anger can also lead to physical conditions like heart disease or cancer, or mental and emotional disorders, especially if bitterness is involved. For example, King Saul ended up mentally ill from his anger, jealousy, and envy of David. He believed David was a threat and pursued him nonstop to kill him (1 Samuel 18:6–11, 19:1–15, 23:15). All Saul's efforts were for naught, for his actions eventually destroyed him (1 Samuel 31:4) and David became king over Judah (2 Samuel 2:7). Anger can also have residual effects. Sadly, many lives are destroyed by a lawsuit, arrest, job and income loss, broken relationships, loss of freedom, wealth, or reputation because of one ill-advised act that is not well thought out.

9. **Anger is in our culture.**
In particular, Hollywood often sets the tone for our culture. Nowadays, anger and violence are popular themes found in many movies and television programs. Anger, especially when intertwined with perceived personal injustice, gives way for personal revenge to be meted out. In fact, when was the last time you watched a movie or television program where you heard: "*. . . vengeance is mine saith the Lord*" or even "*turn the other cheek.*" How about never.

And sometimes, this bleeds over into our society. There are many news stories of a misguided few taking matters into their own hands by physically attacking others, damaging property, rioting, etc. They think they will get away with it without due regard for the suffering of the innocent victims. But make no mistake, there is a higher authority to which all of us are accountable for deeds done in this life.

The heart is the most deceitful above all things,
And desperately wicked. (Jeremiah 17:9 NKJV)

On the other hand, evil behavior, immoral acts, and crime should not be that much of a surprise here; it is certainly not a new theme. It was also like this right before the great flood. Actually, it was worse! And God held all those people to account (they perished), but He thankfully spared those of faith (Noah and his family) (Genesis 6:5–8). We are not quite there yet, but it seems we are headed hurriedly on a similar path.

10. **Not all anger is wrong.**
Are you surprised? Obviously, God gave us the ability to be angry. But why? I believe He gave it to us predominantly to respond to wrongs and injustice. It is undoubtedly natural for us to be mad, given certain situations—being falsely accused, cheated, lied to, etc. If we see an injustice or destructive behavior taking place, it might spur us into action to right a wrong. This is crucial to understand because it also reflects one reason for God's anger. An instance of this is when Jesus was in the temple and confronted those displaying misguided and wrong behavior (John 2:13–16).

11. **We need to understand that God desires to lead and take care of us.**
As the Good Shepherd, He is here to provide and protect us (Psalm 23:1; Psalm 95:7). If we do not understand this, we will invariably follow others

who aren't necessarily looking out for our best interests, but their own. They can act like shepherds but are just another sheep leading other sheep over a cliff. And without God, it can lead one through an unending revolving door of different people with the "right" answer.

Therefore, if we consider looking to God for our every *need*, He will surely provide what we *need*. However, many times in life, people aren't happy with this and can become angry because their *wants* (not *needs*) are not met.

> *For this reason I say to you, do not be worried about your life, as to what you will eat or what you will drink; nor for your body, as to what you will put on. Is not life more than food, and the body more than clothing? Look at the birds of the air, that they do not sow, nor reap nor gather into barns, and yet your heavenly Father feeds them. Are you not worth much more than they? And who of you by being worried can add a single hour to his life?* (Matthew 6:25–27 NASB)

One desire, particularly a desire for justice, can make people mad if not met. However, when we accept God's righteousness, justice, and timing, we can receive much-needed peace, knowing He controls the situation and will deal with it.

There is a popular saying: "Let go. Let God." This answers a predominant question of who is in charge of our lives: us or God? If it truly is God, then absolute joy can come into our lives. Indeed, one can only find this joy through God's Holy Spirit and the fruit made available to us. It starts with love, builds on six more characteristics, and interestingly winds up with self-control:

> But the fruit of the Spirit is love, joy, peace, forbearance, kindness, goodness, faithfulness, gentleness and self-control. (Galatians 5:22–23 NIV)

All are needed to live a more abundant life. For this reason, let the Holy Spirit guide you in all matters.

Let go. Let God.

SECTION TWO

THE ANGER
PROBLEM

CHAPTER 4

CAIN AND REJECTION

(Genesis 4:2–15)

Now Cain said to his brother Abel,
"Let's go out to the field." While they were in the field,
Cain attacked his brother Abel and killed him.

(Genesis 4:8 NIV)

Context

The story of Cain slaying Abel is notorious. Still, we might gloss over this singular evil act without genuinely understanding its implications for us today and throughout history. Truth be told, most of us are accustomed to and often fascinated by news about death of all kinds. Reading about one more death isn't such a big deal, right? In this case, however, it should be because murder can be set apart from other types of death, as it possesses several unique elements:

1. It is high on the scale of sinful acts (one of the Ten Commandments).
2. By its horrendous nature, it is the destruction of another human made in God's image.
3. In most cases, it is preceded by anger, followed by hatred and rage.

As we look at the following story, it begs several questions: Is this about some angry hothead that could not control his anger, and therefore ended up committing the first murder? Or is there something insidious deep within each of us that causes us to have ill will toward others, to the point of doing them harm? What makes a person cross a line and choose a path of evil, while others prefer a path of good? Is it solely anger, or is it anger mixed with other ingredients that may cause an evil deed to occur?

By carefully and insightfully reviewing Cain's life—who he was as a person, his subsequent behavior, and where he went wrong—we can all learn from this story. We have an opportunity to identify measures that will allow us to act prudentially when we face a hot button situation rather than choose an act with a painful outcome, as Cain did.

Biblical Background
(Genesis 3–4:1)

From the beginning of humankind, we find that a common theme is that man repeatedly falls; Cain being no exception. After the original sin, Adam and Eve were cast out of the Garden of Eden. Recall how they listened to Satan (the serpent) and his lies rather than obey God. Both had been disobedient, eating from the tree of knowledge after being told not to. When they did, the difference between good and evil was made known. Therefore, God banished them before they also ate of the tree of life and became like God.

The impact of this first sin has had effects throughout history. When women experience labor, it is *painful*. And for man? The ground was cursed, and man was to have *painful* toil all the days of his life. Notice that life for both men and women, to this day, has not exactly been pain-free.

Eventually, Eve conceived and bore her first two children, Cain and Abel. Admittedly, we do not know the exact ages of Cain or Abel at the time of this story, but they would have lived life for some time, maturing together into men. Because Cain was the firstborn, perhaps he had more of a leadership role, whereas Abel and others would follow. Like their parents, both were given free will to choose between right and wrong, and they also had a personal relationship with God.

The Story

They were no longer in the Garden of Eden, but we may assume the land around it was still quite fertile,

for both farming crops and raising livestock to provide for their needs. Cain worked the ground while
his younger brother, Abel, tended livestock. Indeed,
both Cain's and his brother's free will came into play
because they made offerings to God. It appears they
were to give their best, a small demand based on all
they had been given by Him. Just as God had requested
of Adam, would Adam's children also obey Him? We
know Abel did. He gave back to God, his best, from the
firstborn of his animals. Cain gave fruit from his land.
However, it was not the best.

Although God received Abel's offering with *favor*,
Cain's offering was received with *disfavor*; since he
had chosen not to give his best. Perhaps he wanted
to keep it for himself, or he didn't like to be told
what to do, or maybe he didn't even care. But because
God chose to look at Cain's offering with displeasure,
Cain's sole reaction to God was anger.

The Anger Problem

Cain wasn't just angry; he was riled! His face reflected
as much, for he was sulky and brooding. This anger
went down to his very soul, mixed with all sorts of
negative feelings. Discouraged and feeling dejected,
maybe Cain also thought God had disrespected and
offended him since God had accepted Abel's offering but not his. This probably led to further resentment and hatred. Hadn't Cain given to the Lord?
Yes, but not in total obedience. Hadn't Cain done

what God wanted? No, he did not provide the best he could have, as God requested. Did God further reject Cain? No, God refused the disobedient act, but not the person. However, Cain could not see past his hard-heartedness.

God, showing His love for Cain and wanting him to do better, advises him to do the right thing, as his brother had. Certainly, it was not too late for Cain to correct the error of his way. With a little more time and effort, Cain could present another offering to please God. We find here that God is compassionate and caring for Cain and gives him a second chance. For assuredly, God is the God of second chances. In the same way, didn't He do that with his parents, Adam and Eve, when they were disobedient?

When speaking to Cain, God says all will be well, but Cain needs to do the right thing by giving the first-fruits. It is a simple request to provide the best to God, not the second best or third best. This giving of the firstfruit continues throughout the Bible and is still with us today (Proverbs 3:9-10). We should give the best of ourselves through our time, talents, service, ministry, monetary donations, etc. Why? Because when we do, we honor God and can make a difference in others' lives. And we, in turn, will be blessed!

Earlier, I offered possible reasons why Cain didn't provide his first and best to God. Well, we can ask the same question of ourselves. Do we also give the first and best to God? Like Cain, maybe we are untrusting, selfish, ungrateful, or don't want to honor God. When we give less than our best, it can show our true feelings and where our eyes are focused: ourselves or God.

Cain had done wrong, and God pointed this out like any loving parent would do to correct willful behavior. Cain was about to experience what his parents had gone through—doing wrong, getting caught, and then paying for it.

The Anger Response

Now, in this "worked up" emotional state of mind, Cain stews about the situation. He is mad, jealous of his brother, and hurt from being rejected. Cain's pride also gets in the way and hinders his ability to emulate his brother's actions and receive God's acceptance. To be sure, self comes into play here. Self-love, arrogance, and self-glorification are the central focus of pride. A pride-filled person has a hard time admitting to wrongdoing. One will eventually falter, trip, and fall with contempt leading to destruction (Proverbs 16:18). And so, God gives him a warning:

> But if you do not do what is right, sin is crouching at your door; it desires to have you, but you must rule over it. (Genesis 4:7 NIV)

Nevertheless, Cain does not do the right thing, falls into temptation, and chooses to sin. This is undoubtedly the most pivotal moment in Cain's life. Rather than take it all in, reflect on his mistake, and remedy it, he shuts the gate to the path God has asked him to take. Cain proceeds in another direction altogether, and with a hardened heart, he plans his revenge: if God rejects him, then Cain will reject his brother (and through him, God).

Indeed, sin is crouching at the door for all of us. Like Cain, we too must heed God's warning. In the same manner, sin is like a lion on the prowl, hunched over and hidden in the bushes. It is always stalking us and waiting to spring into action. It pounces on its often-unsuspecting victim swiftly and is almost always deadly, for it wants to destroy (1 Peter 5:8). Here, it does.

Cain continues to stew in his anger, like a simmering soup getting hotter. Unable in his mind to tolerate the situation any longer and at the same time not doing it God's way, he does it his way:

1. Cain rejects God's advice.
2. He gives in to temptation.
3. He crosses the line into sin.

With his heart full of rebellion, Cain is now bent on a path of destruction!

Cain has now allowed anger to morph into hatred. All judgment is clouded. He fixates on one thing alone: punish his brother. We do not know if Cain intended to kill his brother that day or if he even understood what death was, for no one had died before, let alone been murdered. Perhaps he had an inkling of death based on his brother's sacrifices of animals. Maybe Cain only wanted to scare his brother and do him some harm, but we will never know. In the end, he commits multiple sins. Cain deceives his brother, kills him, and then lies to God, all the while attempting to cover up his crime, thinking that he will get away with it.

So Cain cleverly lulls his brother into a false sense of security by putting on an act. Innocent Abel, who trusts him completely, suspects nothing and has no reason to fear for his life, for why should he? This is his older brother, who he cares for and respects. Usually, the firstborn leads and the second born follows without question or hesitancy. Abel is God-fearing, faithful, loyal, obedient, and innocently trusts his brother.

Abel, taken by surprise, is murdered. Innocent Abel, who only did right in God's eyes, is now gone, slain by his brother. He is never to take another breath, never to see one more sunrise, never to see his parents again, and never to have children himself. He will never love and be loved back ever again. Good, obedient Abel is now dead.

Not as Cain, who was of that wicked one, and slew his brother. And wherefore slew he him? Because his own works were evil, and his brother's righteous. (1 John 3:12 KJV)

Abel is a victim, to be sure. But Cain has not thought out the impact on himself, his parents, or other siblings. Because murder is not a victimless crime; it has repercussions for all. It changes the lives of the murderer, the murdered, and the community. In this case, the family of the murderer and the family of the murdered are the same. Adam and Eve would now have to lose two of their children. Abel was dead, and soon Cain would be banished.

The act of murder itself is extreme, for it is absolute. No doubt, Cain believes he has gotten away with murder, but he hasn't. To Cain's surprise, God finds him and wants to ask him a couple of questions. Of course, God already knows the answers to both. God then allows Cain an opportunity to come clean and confess his evil deed, like most parents would do when their children do wrong and are caught.

Then the Lord said to Cain, "Where is your brother Abel?" "I don't know," he replied. "Am I my brother's keeper?" The Lord said, "What have you done? Listen! Your brother's blood cries out to me from the ground." (Genesis 4:9−10 NIV)

Cain is confronted, and his web of deceit also comes apart. Like most evildoers attempting to get out of their snare, he then travels down the road of a cover-up. Cain knows where his brother's body is, but lies about it. He does not want to confess his deed. And why should he? Cain is smug, snarly, and combative. He thinks he will get away with it by not telling the truth. Therefore, Cain chooses not to answer the question but to answer God's question with a question. Concealing the truth at all costs is his chosen path, but it is wrong.

After all, Cain is getting to be pretty good at deception, or so he thinks. Didn't Cain try to deceive God earlier with his offering, not to mention setting a trap for his brother? Cain, now in self-deception mode, believes he will get away with murder and evades the question. He then attempts to deceive God one more time. There are two aspects in play here.

The first is that Cain is vain and puffed up with pride. He can do no wrong because his own "superiority" defines right and wrong. But with pride goes haughtiness, which frequently leads to disobedience. When people believe that they are self-important and think they are above the law, they might disregard laws because they feel that the law does not apply to them.

The second is that Cain followed in his parents' footsteps. Both Adam and Eve sinned by eating the forbidden fruit because they believed they could do their own thing and not get caught. Similar to his parents, Cain sinned and was also found out. And like his parents, he tried to come up with excuses to get out of his guilt.

The Anger Consequences

Cain took no responsibility for his misdeeds. He felt no sense of what would happen to him next, especially God's judgment. But Cain was to find out what justice felt like. To a certain extent, he now changes places with his brother and becomes, in his mind, a victim. God then places Cain under a curse, and he is driven away to be a wanderer. With his punishment in hand, Cain (not so proud anymore) asks God for mercy, which he could not show to his brother, but now wants for himself. So God placed a mark on him so that he would not be killed (Genesis 4:11–16).

God showed not only justice, but also mercy. For his punishment, Cain would never be forgotten as a murderer. Anyone who looked upon him would be reminded of his deed. They would know Cain's true character: violent, angry, and hate-filled. We are not told if anyone sought revenge on Cain or if he lived a long life. We know he married and had children, all because of God's mercy.

As a result of his punishment, Cain probably had to look over his shoulder for the rest of his life, knowing anybody might kill him in a moment. Thus, he probably lived out his life paranoid and suspicious, never trusting or being trusted as his brother had trusted him. In the end, rather than give God the firstfruits, Cain would attempt to toil for the rest of his days, with the sad fact of producing no fruit.

Cain's infamous act was permanent and forever written in history. Cain thought he would get away with it—the perfect murder. He thought about it and acted on it. Interestingly, didn't Cain consider that with Abel's disappearance, and because Cain was the last one with him, there might be questions asked? What was the story he was going to tell his parents? Or to God? Whatever it was, it would be a lie.

There is no indication that Cain ever confessed. Cain became an outcast with a mark upon him, living restlessly for the remainder of his days. In the end, the one who wanted to be the first was indeed the first—the first murderer!

Hot Buttons

Cain had many buttons that were pushed. The two most significant were the inability to **obey authority** and to **receive criticism or correction**. Just as important was not being **number one (pride)** and believing falsely that God was **rejecting** and **insulting** him. Cain had two more buttons: **getting caught in sin** and being **asked to confess it** (which he refused). Taken individually, perhaps he might have coped better, but when these buttons were combined, it made for an insensitive and callous person who acted angrily and without regret.

Points to Ponder

Beware of Satan's wiles. This story is the continuation of the fall. In the aftermath of the Garden of Eden, this was the next round in the battle of good versus evil. Previously, Satan (that same serpent in the garden) wanted to take God's throne, rebelled, and was cast out of heaven with many other rebellious angels (Ezekiel 28:12–19; Isaiah 14:12–14; Revelation 12:4, 7–9).

After successfully tempting the parents, Satan's next target was their children. We saw how Cain was a very proud person with evil desires. Presumably, Satan knew this. Thus, he could get to Cain to destroy his brother (and to a lesser degree, Cain himself). Though Satan is a defeated foe, it doesn't mean he won't relentlessly continue to attack all believers. We need to be continually on guard for Satan and his schemes of luring us away from God through lies and deception (John 8:44).

Anger is part of our sinful nature. Part of being human is this sinful nature warring continually within. We must fight it when tempted to be overwhelmed with anger. Each of us has choices every day to do the right thing or the wrong thing and, at the same time, to follow God or not follow Him.

Therefore do not let sin reign in your mortal body so that you obey its evil desires. Do not offer any part of yourself to sin as an instrument of wickedness, but rather offer yourselves to God as those who have been brought from death to life; and offer every part of yourself to him as an instrument of righteousness. (Romans 6:12–13 NIV)

When tempted to become angry, there is always a way out. Cain had several viable options but ultimately chose murder. His entire life changed with one deadly blow. His actions solved nothing. There are several ways to fight temptation and the trouble it may bring. We can capture the thought and give it to God. We can take up God's Word and quote Bible verses and pray. And if necessary, we can walk away. Remember, God will ensure we get through, no matter the situation we might be in or how we feel, including being angry.

No temptation has overtaken you except what is common to mankind. And God is faithful; he will not let you be tempted beyond what you can bear. But when you are tempted, he will also provide a way out so that you can endure it. (1 Corinthians 10:13 NIV)

Thankfully, if we fall into temptation and end up sinning, we can repent, ask for forgiveness, and receive it (1 John 1:9).

It is wiser to ignore a slight. When God rejected his offering, Cain felt slighted, which contributed to his jealousy and anger. He wanted to be noticed. Cain's most significant problems were being thin-skinned and the inability to accept constructive criticism, which often go hand in hand. Cain had many hot buttons, and because he confronted none of them, he never resolved them. In time, they built up until they ended in an evil act. Fortunately, and thankfully, it's not too late to identify and work out our hot buttons.

Cain got what he wanted—attention! God made sure that others would always notice Cain by a permanent mark. Yes, God could have taken Cain's life for taking Abel's. Instead, He showed him mercy and allowed him to live. In retrospect, it all started because Cain would not let go of what he believed was an insult, and worse, didn't deal with it wisely.

A person's wisdom yields patience; it is to one's glory to overlook an offense. (Proverbs 19:11 NIV)

Anger blocks out rational thinking and reasonable conduct. Anger can allow for irrational thinking. But be warned, it can also lead to irrational behavior. In Cain's case, evil thought produced evil behavior. So guard your thoughts well.

For from within, out of the heart of men, proceed the evil thoughts, fornications, thefts, murders, adulteries . . . (Mark 7:21 NASB)

Pride goes before disgrace. Perhaps like Cain, we also want to do things our way, possibly because of stubbornness. But in pursuing accolades, we too might be disgraced. In Cain's case, he not only was humiliated forever but he also wore his disgrace. Therefore, it is wiser to be humble and sensible than a fool headed for embarrassment and shame.

> *When pride comes, then comes disgrace, but with humility comes wisdom.* (Proverbs 11:2 NIV)

When angry, it is all right to reach out and share with others how you feel. Rather than keeping things bottled up inside, Cain could have talked to someone: his parents, his brother, his other siblings, or even God Himself. But he was unwilling to express himself constructively and talk about his issues, which led to a limited and shortsighted remedy. Unfortunately, because all his options came from within, he could not receive counsel and advice from others for the best way forward.

> *The way of a fool is right in his own eyes, But a wise man is he who listens to counsel.* (Proverbs 12:15 NASB)

Anger can reflect a lack of faith and trust. One of the reasons Cain became angry was because he lacked faith and confidence in God. Without faith, it is not possible to please God (Hebrews 11:6). It appears Cain never really gave God a chance to be trusted. It also looks like he did not trust anyone but himself. It isn't easy to believe in someone if you do not trust them. Do you have faith in God? Abel, on the other hand, trusted God in faith and obedience. Therefore, he desired to please God by presenting the best that he could offer. Do you offer God your best?

> *By faith Abel offered to God a better sacrifice than Cain, through which he obtained the testimony that he was righteous, God testifying about his gifts . . .* (Hebrews 11:4 NASB)

With faith and trust comes peace. Cain was forever restless. After being banished, he not only had to be on guard in the daytime but in the nighttime as well. Lacking faith in God, he would never know true peace. Do you have peace with God?

> *Therefore, having been justified by faith, we have peace with God through our Lord Jesus Christ.* (Romans 5:1 NASB)

Anger can lead to further abuse and violence. The acts coming from anger can worsen over time when not put in check. One often sees this in negative and inappropriate behaviors from emotional abuse or physical violence. For the most part, if a person can calm down, even after becoming angry, they are better positioned to reason out a more moderate path and therefore avert an argument or any future bad behavior. In Cain's case, it is questionable he learned this valuable lesson after being banished.

A hot-tempered person stirs up conflict, but the one who is patient calms a quarrel. (Proverbs 15:18 NIV)

Anger can lead to disobeying authority. Cain didn't want to listen to or obey God. We too can turn away from godly wisdom and counsel because we think we know better. Have you ever been instructed by someone in authority or someone else who cares about you? If correction is not taken to heart, there is usually a cost to pay, perhaps in the form of losing out on a blessing and a probable repeat of disobedient behavior.

But prove yourselves doers of the word, and not merely hearers who delude themselves. For if anyone is a hearer of the word and not a doer, he is like a man who looks at his natural face in a mirror; for once he has looked at himself and gone away, he has immediately forgotten what kind of person he was. But one who looks intently at the perfect law, the law of liberty, and abides by it, not having become a forgetful hearer but an effectual doer, this man will be blessed in what he does. (James 1:22–25 NASB)

Consider how your actions today will affect your future. In the end, rather than love and protect Abel, Cain chose not to be his brother's keeper. Instead, he chose to become his brother's assailant, full of betrayal and deceit.

Therefore, choose a righteous path with long-term ramifications and an eternal home: heaven. That truly is where our hearts should be with our eyes ever looking up.

> *Do not store up for yourselves treasures on earth, where moth and rust destroy, and where thieves break in and steal. But store up for yourselves treasures in heaven, where neither moth nor rust destroys, and where thieves do not break in or steal; for where your treasure is, there your heart will be also.* (Matthew 6:19–21 NASB)

CHAPTER 5

MOSES AND PERSONAL (IN) JUSTICE

(Exodus 1-2)

One day, after Moses had grown up, he went out
to where his own people were and watched them
at their hard labor. He saw an Egyptian beating a Hebrew,
one of his own people. Looking this way and that
and seeing no one, he killed the Egyptian
and hid him in the sand.

(Exodus 2:11–12 NIV)

Context

Moses was a great man of faith and is revered in both the Christian and Jewish religions. He was chosen by God, even as an infant, and later used in a powerful way to deliver God's people out of bondage. During his lifetime, Moses played many roles: Egyptian prince, Midian shepherd, archrival to the Pharaoh, national leader, prophet, judge, and warrior. Also, as a gifted writer, he is recognized as the author of the

Pentateuch (the first five Bible books). Finally, Moses is known as the Hebrews' deliverer, lawgiver, and for having entered into the Mosaic covenant with God.

Despite all these accomplishments, Moses had one glaring weakness—a lack of self-control that caused anger issues throughout his life. Although Moses was nothing like Cain, anger was common to both of them. In Moses's case, he displayed several instances of not maintaining control. He killed an Egyptian (Exodus 2:12), broke the tablets God had given him (Exodus 32:19), and struck a rock for water (Numbers 20:10–11).

Moses's life can be a reminder to each of us that if we are not on guard constantly, we may succumb to a sudden angry moment. Even though we might successfully manage our anger one day, it is no guarantee that we will do the same on any other.

For some, including myself, anger management may be a lifelong struggle. If and when we do get mad, we need to remember there are always consequences, even if we believe that the anger is "justified." Moses's story is an excellent example of this.

Biblical Background

Beginning with Abraham, God had made several promises to the Hebrews as a chosen and free people. As the first patriarch, Abraham was a man of incredible faith who honored God, and in turn, God honored and blessed him. Subsequently, Abraham fathered Isaac, who then became the father of Jacob (later to be named Israel). Israel had twelve sons who then had families of their own, later becoming the twelve tribes of the nation of Israel. Fortunately, God sent one son, Joseph, to Egypt, saving his brothers from famine.

Moses would later be born there in Egypt into the tribe of Levi, his lineage going back to Abraham. Just as God had set Abraham and Joseph apart in leadership roles, He would do the same for Moses and his brother Aaron, who would later lead the Levitical priesthood. The priests would play a significant role in the worshiping of God. Although at the time of Moses's birth the blessing of his forefathers might have appeared to be gone, God was still moving.

The Story

To begin, the Hebrews initially lived alongside the Egyptians without issue. Eventually, however, the Egyptians became their masters, which lasted hundreds of years and over many generations. No longer free, they were property; this meant day-to-day hardship with possible punishment. They were put to work as skilled brickmakers and builders. If they did not meet their quotas of bricks, their enslavers would exact "justice." This was the world Moses was born into.

At the time of his birth, there was a proclamation by an evil Pharaoh to rid Egypt of all Hebrew baby boys. The midwives were to drown them by throwing them into the Nile River. This was done because of the widely held belief that the ever-increasing number of Hebrews would eventually rebel against the Egyptians.

To protect Moses, his mother placed him in a basket and floated him down the Nile. He was saved by Pharaoh's daughter: "She named him Moses, saying, 'I drew him out of the water'" (Exodus 2:10 NIV). Because of the actions of these two loving women, he escaped an early death. Eventually growing up as a prince, Moses was accorded rank and status and lived a privileged and comfortable life. He certainly would have known that the Hebrews were enslaved, and that the Egyptians were their masters.

Despite being in the middle of all this hardship, the Hebrews still possessed hope. They worshiped the one true living God who had previously blessed their ancestors. On the other hand, the Egyptians did not know the living God because they worshiped many gods and goddesses through physical and inanimate idols. In the same vein, the Egyptians built many structures (like the pyramids, Sphinx, etc.) to commemorate and memorialize their leaders and glorify their religion and culture. However, Moses would reject all of this, especially their faith. The truth he sought was not to be found among their many gods or goddesses. Instead, he would find it in the one true God of the Hebrews.

The Anger Problem

Embracing his Hebrew background, Moses saw the injustice wherever he turned. Although his entire kinfolk was enslaved, maybe he thought he could play a small role in protecting at least one Hebrew. In truth, if we came face-to-face with such cruelty and subjugation, many of us would be morally outraged, and some would step in to stop it. Moses did precisely that—he stepped in, but he went too far.

The Anger Response

Moses came to the rescue to right what he believed was wrong. He acted quickly and decisively and stopped the beating of one of his brethren. As a result, he killed an Egyptian. Like Cain, thinking he would get away with it, it didn't go as planned. In this case, there were other Hebrew witnesses. Given his circumstances, could Moses have chosen another path? What were the options before Moses?

1. Do nothing and walk away? *That would not resolve any future beatings.*
2. Talk to the enslaver and try to reason with him? *But what could he say?*
3. Report the enslaver? *But to whom and for what?*

4. Based on his royal relationship, speak directly to the Pharaoh to stop this captivity altogether. *But wouldn't the answer be an emphatic no?*

5. Why not just take matters into his own hands? *And with it, immediately solve the injustice (so he believed).*

Thus, Moses decided to solve it on the spot with violence. It also begs the question: did he desire to kill the Egyptian or just stop him? We will never know because the act ended in death. This is true of all acts of violence; one never knows how it will turn out.

The Anger Consequence

With the deed committed, giving himself up and pleading his case would not be an option. Therefore, to cover his tracks, Moses went about his business. In a short while, Pharaoh would find out about the killing and hunt him. In Pharaoh's eyes, it was not an act of rescue.

The Hebrew individual who was beaten was also in a precarious, if not dangerous, position. Perhaps his life was forfeited too because Pharaoh would have sought his own "justice" and would have been angered not to catch Moses. In the end, many were probably affected: the Hebrew (and possibly others), the Egyptian, Moses, and their respective families.

Moses, a prince no more, became a murderer running for his life. With a death sentence hanging over his head, he fled. To stay alive, he kept moving and crossed the Egyptian desert. He eventually ended up in Midian, hundreds of miles east of Egypt, where Mt. Sinai is located. It is certain that God watched over and protected him.

God knew Moses at birth, as a youngster, as he grew into manhood, and in his later years. Moses's heart always appeared to be in the right place. He was faithful to God and His people, and God was faithful to Moses. This story gives us hope that God can still use any of us no matter what we have done, good or bad. It comes down to where we place our faith. Still, could God have used Moses if the killing did not happen? I believe the answer is yes.

> By faith Moses, when he had grown up, refused to be called the son of Pharaoh's daughter, choosing rather to endure ill-treatment with the people of God than to enjoy the passing pleasures of sin, considering the reproach of Christ greater riches than the treasures of Egypt; for he was looking to the reward. By faith he left Egypt, not fearing the wrath of the king; for he endured, as seeing Him who is unseen. (Hebrews 11:24–27 NASB)

Over the next forty years and away from Egypt, Moses became the head of his own family and became a highly experienced shepherd. He gained the necessary knowledge and skill set to lead God's people successfully out of Egypt and survive the rigors of the wilderness. But beforehand, at Mt. Sinai, Moses would meet God in the form of a burning bush (Exodus 3:4). As a result of this face-to-face encounter, Moses would transform and grow in faith, wisdom, and stature. God used Moses spectacularly and powerfully to free His people from Egypt (Deuteronomy 34:11).

Hot Buttons

In Moses's case, he had two major buttons. The first was for a perceived **injustice** at the hands of the Egyptian(s). The second was if someone crossed his **moral boundary.** He became outraged, indignant, and a hothead when these happened. But he also paid for it (e.g., running for his life, etc.). Although not perfect, he did have a firm moral compass and strong will. And because he served God faithfully, He also blessed him accordingly.

Points to Ponder

Anger can often cause quick responses. People with tempers can react rashly, immediately, and decisively, rather than taking a breath, calming down, and thinking things over. This often results in very destructive and long-lasting consequences, not only to the recipient of the anger but also to the one dishing it out.

If you ever have been in or have known someone in an abusive relationship, some scars may last a lifetime and affect future behavior and relationships. To be clear, you and I are not accountable for how others act or how they act out! That is on them and not on you. But it is still incumbent upon each of us, especially during heated times, to curb our emotions and act appropriately.

> *Do not be quickly provoked in your spirit, for anger resides in the lap of fools.* (Ecclesiastes 7:9 NIV)

Taking justice into your own hands, whether justified or not, has consequences. Barring extraordinary situations, it is much wiser not to seek justice yourself. Instead, put them in God's hands and involve law enforcement if need be. This will allow God to work it out, protect in the interim, and eventually have justice carried out. And while self-defense laws allow for protecting oneself and others against imminent harm, one should always exercise the greatest prudence.

> *The Lord is a refuge for the oppressed, a stronghold in times of trouble.* (Psalm 9:9 NIV)

Managing anger may be a lifetime effort. Moses is an excellent example of anger management as a lifetime endeavor. When Moses was much older, he became angry with God's people because of their disobedience. He broke the same tablets given to him by God to instruct them on obedience (Exodus 32:19).

Later, while still in the desert, Moses was the one who became disobedient, striking a rock in anger to get water for His people. For that outburst, God did not allow him to enter the Promised Land (Numbers 20:10–12).

Again, Moses shows us that the temptation of anger can visit any of us at any time. Especially when in those stress-filled and anxious moments, it may lead to a confrontation. But we can choose our reaction.

Fools give full vent to their rage, but the wise bring calm in the end. (Proverbs 29:11 NIV)

God can allow good to come out of a bad situation. Besides Moses, the following are some of God's people who were in precarious situations they themselves caused, yet God still redeemed them and used each one in His service.

Isaac lied to the Philistine king to conceal his marriage. God used him to continue to bless the Abrahamic line (Genesis 26).

Jacob deceived many, including his father Isaac (Genesis 27). God blessed him with many sons who would later become the tribes of Israel (Genesis 35; Numbers 1).

Samson was the last of the Israelite judges and turned away from God. He called out to God, received his strength back, and destroyed the Philistine enemies in their temple (Judges 16).

David committed adultery with Bathsheba, and to cover it up he murdered her husband (2 Samuel 11). God used him as the King of Israel and Judah for many more years to come (1 Kings 2).

Jonah, the prophet, ran away from God. He ended up sparking a revival in Nineveh (Jonah 1, 3).

Peter denied Jesus (John 18). He later became the leader of the early Christian church (Acts 1).

Paul persecuted many new believers in Christ (Acts 9). As an apostle, he became perhaps the greatest of missionaries (Acts 13–28).

All the preceding individuals received grace and mercy from God, no matter what they had done. Because of his faith, Moses received God's grace and mercy and went on to do great things for Him. In the same way, whatever our life stories are, we too can be used by God to do great things for Him.

CHAPTER 6

SAUL AND DISOBEDIENCE

(1 Samuel 12–31)

Saul was very angry; this refrain displeased him greatly.
"They have credited David with tens of thousands,"
he thought, "but me with only thousands.
What more can he get but the kingdom?"

(1 Samuel 18:8 NIV)

Context

Picture this: You are one of the best-looking people around, with height and a physique to boot. Now, add fame and wealth to that, and what a mixture for success! To many, these characteristics define a person's chance for success, acceptance, and approval. Why would anyone possessing these desired qualities end up literally falling on their sword? Yet this is exactly what happened to Saul, Israel's first king. But as we shall see, many achievements in our lives can

often end up being meaningless if they are without
God's guidance.

Saul, like many other biblical figures, started with
promise and had potential for greatness. Unfortunately,
as he ruled over his kingdom for over forty years, he
became spiritually bankrupt and mentally and emotionally unstable. Saul spiraled out of control by making poor choices and failing to trust the One who
appointed him king in the first place—God. One of
his most careless choices was when he disobeyed the
prophet Samuel at the battle of Gilgal (1 Samuel 13:13–
14), thereby jeopardizing His kingship.

That other was David, who became a hero by slaying Goliath and defeating the Philistines. Appointed
high in the military ranks, David was successful at all
undertakings. In a public outpouring, people danced
and sang, "'Saul has slain his thousands, and David
his tens of thousands.'" (1 Samuel 18:7 NIV)

Eventually, Saul no longer believed he was number
one in his subjects' eyes and saw David as a threat,
setting up an imagined rivalry for the remainder of
his days. As we shall see shortly, this ongoing resentment came about because of what he had done earlier
at Gilgal, which led to continued reckless disregard
and defiance toward God.

Saul's life story can teach us about the relationship between disobedience and anger. Living a life

of waywardness, beset with all sorts of calamity and turmoil, Saul never realized that there might have been a better plan for his life. Had he repented and asked for forgiveness of the one true King, God, his life might have been different. Fortunately, it is not too late for us. He truly is a loving and forgiving God; we only need to ask.

Biblical Background

For many centuries, Judges had led Israel, beginning with Joshua and others like Deborah. Nevertheless, God was always their true leader and King. The Israelites, however, were not satisfied with this arrangement and made a clamor. They wanted a human king, like those of other lands. At the time, Samuel had led the country for many years as a judge and prophet. At God's direction, Samuel now sought out the first man–king to give the people what they desired. Therefore, God gave the people exactly what they wanted. But it came with a stern warning:

> *Only fear the Lord and serve Him in truth with all your heart; for consider what great things He has done for you. But if you still do wickedly, both you and your king will be swept away.* (1 Samuel 12:24–25 NASB)

The Story

Saul was God's choice to lead as the new king. He was a thirty-year-old man from the tribe of Benjamin.

Saul was born with exceptional looks and stood head and shoulders above everybody else (1 Samuel 9:2). Because of lifelong flattery, it is possible Saul believed he could do no wrong. And once king, who would argue with him?

Although Saul had strengths, his faults were many—including an overabundance of vanity, stubbornness, and envy. At the core of Saul's persona was his self-ishness, defiance, and mistrust of God. The combination of these failings led to an explosive mixture that would end in Saul's ruin.

The Anger Problem

Forty years after coming out of Egypt, the Israelites entered Canaan, the Promised Land. However, settling there caused friction with its inhabitants, particularly the Philistines, who would become their continual enemies (Joshua 13). That was still the case when Saul was king. As one battle neared at Gilgal, the Philistines were highly confident with their massive army, including thousands of chariots.

Saul's outnumbered troops became restless, seeing the enormity of the task ahead and their lives on the line. On that day, their courage evaporated, and some even deserted. Saul was also fearful and believed that victory was in jeopardy if he didn't act quickly. Samuel had directed Saul to wait for him to make offerings to God. Rather than trust Samuel and wait, Saul disobeyed and made the offerings himself. Because of this act, Samuel told Saul that he would lose his kingdom (1 Samuel 13). Later, when handed the victory by God, Saul would still not place his complete trust in Him; seeing was not believing.

Likewise, Saul was given other opportunities to do the right thing but did not. For example, he did not wipe out the Amalekites when charged to do so. This pattern of faithlessness and refusal to obey God would mark Saul throughout his kingship. Though Saul could command, he would not be commanded. And in the case of disobedience with the Amalekites, it resulted in God further rejecting him. Saul would never be the same (1 Samuel 15).

The Anger Response

As time passed, Saul's decision-making became more and more rash and unsteady. When things didn't go his way, especially when they favored David, Saul became angry. An evil spirit, likely demonic oppression, came upon him, and he tried to kill David with a spear (1 Samuel 18:10–11). This hatred toward David led Saul to hunt him down and try to kill him several more times (1 Samuel 19:1–15, 23:15).

Saul then suffered extreme mood swings and perhaps even madness. Evil forces undoubtedly influenced him, but primarily, he lived a life of transgression toward God. His continued unrepentance and disobedience prompted him to seek a medium to speak to the now-dead Samuel. This descent into spiritual darkness and depression started with insubordination and uncontrolled jealousy. More acts of defiance followed, for he was unwilling to control himself and turn from his rebellious ways.

The Anger Consequence

Disobedience would continue to mark Saul's reign. One may argue that because some things came too quickly for him, such as the crown, self-reliance went to Saul's head. This would explain his self-centeredness. However, he never really understood that much success comes through one's merits and where one's heart is toward God (David had both). Saul was never genuinely thankful for all the blessings God had bestowed on him. And when things didn't go his way, he tended to lose control.

Even though Saul was aware that his kingdom was at stake, he continued to commit unwise acts, leading him further and further away from God. Perhaps he didn't believe God and His Word. Saul also disregarded good counsel, seeking evil counsel instead, possibly thinking he could take back control of his life. This only led him on a path full of darkness. Saul could no longer see the light to guide him. Spiritually blinded, he didn't go to the one Source that could have helped him—God. Subsequently, troubled, in pain and agony, and without his family, Saul ended his life and reign by falling on his sword. Although Saul had a great start, he went astray and finished tragically—proud, defiant, and unrepentant to the end.

Hot Buttons

Saul had several buttons. He neither **trusted** God nor **obeyed** Him. Perhaps His most prominent button was **resentment** toward another person—David. Saul (in his eyes) was publicly **humiliated, rejected, and feared the loss of status.** Unfortunately, the conjured-up rivalry took up much of Saul's energy and led to a consuming effort to destroy David while crippling Saul emotionally and mentally.

Points to Ponder

Anger (with disobedience) can often limit our spiritual life. Many times, these two work together and reinforce each other with unfortunate results. At first, Saul was spiritually mindful of the instruction and guidance of God, and he even prophesied. But over time, he slipped into a false sense of self-worth, turned away from God, and got angry when he didn't get his way. Saul probably thought, why obey God if He's not needed or wanted? Perhaps he also cared more about the trappings of the world. In his lofty position as king, Saul could go his own way without needing approval from anyone, including God.

Many things can divert us from spiritual matters, overshadow our relationship with God, and turn us away from Him. They could be the busyness of life, the pursuit of worldly success, and in our "off" time, being distracted by the digital world of entertainment, gaming, or social media while living in the age of the "virtual" world. Whatever that thing is that could be taking your eyes off God, consider spending more quality time with Him.

Freeing up precious time can allow for studying His Word, praying for others, being with others, or choosing other activities to grow closer to Him. If we do, we can focus on heavenly things above and our eternal home. And if not, like Saul, many things can take us in the wrong direction, causing possible anger and disobedience, often ending in sorrow and regret.

> For those who are according to the flesh set their minds on the things of the flesh, but those who are according to the Spirit, the things of the Spirit. (Romans 8:5 NASB)

Obviously, Saul did not finish well. He continued to stumble by making many bad choices. The path he took was rocky, unsteady, and troubled. Fortunately, we need not go the same way. Paul concludes that we can finish well; by being spirit-filled warriors, doing His will daily, and never losing faith in God.

I have fought the good fight, I have finished the race,
I have kept the faith. (2 Timothy 4:7 NIV)

Anger (with disobedience) leaves no peace. Disobedience can wear a person down. It can increase one's
defensiveness to others, especially if asked about specific sin. Sinning individuals tend to look over their
shoulders to avoid being caught and suffering punishment. This waywardness can put them in a constant state of agitation (and anger) because of the
ever-present fear in them. In Saul's case, the fear that
gripped him was losing his crown.

Subsequently, unforgiveness can lead to restlessness
and not recharging our spiritual batteries. Lacking
peace, a person can get cranky and upset, leading to
a short fuse. For this reason, God forgives, offering
calm in our lives regardless of the situation. We only
need to ask and receive this forgiveness. By doing
this, restoration can take effect with the much-
needed peace that can only come from above.

And the peace of God, which transcends all under-
standing, will guard your hearts and your minds in
Christ Jesus. (Philippians 4:7 NIV)

Anger (with disobedience) is often tied to trust issues.
Saul rarely placed his trust in God. If you don't trust
someone to look out for your best interest, you will tend
not to listen to them. In this case, Saul didn't trust or
listen to God. This contributed significantly to his anger.

After Samuel died, Saul rarely considered others' advice (even though he didn't always listen to Samuel). Instead, Saul leaned heavily on his own experiences, sadly making many more poor choices. As king, these decisions affected the entire nation, which led them down whatever road he took, for good or bad. Eventually, this led to the country's defeat at the hands of the Philistines.

> *Trust in the Lord with all your heart And do not lean on your own understanding. In all your ways acknowledge Him, And He will make your paths straight.* (Proverbs 3:5–6 NASB)

Anger (with foolishness) can make for bad decisions, so pray! Saul was foolish because he made decisions when he was angry. Decisions made in anger are often not wise because they are typically made in extreme haste, with possibly some hostility in mind. If we make decisions when emotional, without considering their consequences, especially eternal ones, we will not make the best choices.

> *He who is slow to anger has great understanding, But he who is quick-tempered exalts folly.* (Proverbs 14:29 NASB)

And pray! If the matter is not prayed over, the likelihood of success will diminish. So pray in all circumstances and all situations, particularly for all critical

life decisions. Make your requests known to God, for
He will work on your behalf to give you only the best.
Had Saul done any of these things, his life would have
turned out differently.

> *And pray in the Spirit on all occasions with all kinds
> of prayers and requests. With this in mind, be alert
> and always keep on praying for all the Lord's people.*
> (Ephesians 6:18 NIV)

CHAPTER 7

HAMAN'S REVENGE

(The Book of Esther)

Haman went out that day happy and in high spirits.
But when he saw Mordecai at the king's gate
and observed that he neither rose nor showed fear
in his presence, he was filled with rage against Mordecai.

(Esther 5:9 NIV)

Context

When one thinks about an angry person, who might come to mind? Would we also connect this anger to evil and the rage and hatred that can sometimes follow? One of the central persons in this story would undoubtedly be up there on an all-time evil list. He was a hater, schemer, destroyer, and certainly could get very, very angry. His name was Haman. He was considered a "wise" man and served his Persian king as a close confidant. In this prominent position, Haman could sway his ruler to make sweeping proclamations affecting many people. One of these was specially done out of revenge to destroy God's people.

Biblical Background

What follows is a short recap of the Jewish people and how they ended up in Persia serving a king under the mastery of one of the evilest of advisers. To begin with, Solomon, one of David's many sons, eventually became king over all of Israel (1 Chronicles 29). Within decades, Israel became divided: Israel to the north and Judah to the south (1 Kings 11). Israel had become less God-oriented, fell into disarray, and subsequently was defeated by the Assyrians (2 Kings 17). Judah then became a vassal state of Babylon (modern-day Iraq) (2 Kings 24).

Within several years, Judah rebelled and was quelled; however, Babylon took many prisoners. Eventually, Babylon conquered Judah and destroyed much of Jerusalem (Jeremiah 39). Later, Babylon was defeated by the Persian Empire (modern-day Iran). Under the Persian King Cyrus, the Jews in Babylon were allowed to return home to resettle and rebuild the destroyed temple in Jerusalem (Ezra 1). There remained, however, a remnant of Jews still living in the Persian Empire.

Sometime later, Xerxes (Ahasuerus) became the Persian king and sought to replace his queen Vashti (Esther 1). At the time, a Jewess named Esther (Hadassah) was raised by her older cousin Mordecai. Under Mordecai's counsel, she would be elevated to the queen's position and be used powerfully by God to save His people (Esther 2). But before that could happen, there was one individual that stood in their way. He was a hothead who was wicked to the core and intent on destroying them. Haman's confrontation with the Jews would end up as a classic battle between good and evil.

The Story

When the edict went forth to replace the former Persian queen, many young women were brought to the palace as candidates. Esther was one of them. Mordecai had told her not to reveal her nationality or background. Loving her as a father, he kept close tabs on her by regularly visiting the courtyard near the harem. For one year, she went through the prescribed beauty treatment. Eventually, she found favor with the king and was crowned his new queen. All the while, Mordecai continued to be near, sitting at the king's gate. While there one day, he heard two guardsmen plotting to assassinate the king and warned Queen Esther. She reported it, and the plot was foiled. The credit went to Mordecai—an event that was added to the official record (Esther 2).

Subsequently, Haman comes on the scene. He too finds favor with the king and is elevated to the highest honor, a seat above all other nobles. Another recognition bestowed upon him was that anyone near the palace gate had to honor him. This would have included Mordecai, who had become a permanent fixture there. Though all honored Haman, Mordecai would not (Esther 3). Those around Mordecai spoke to him, but he still refused to comply, for he told them he was a Jew (Daniel 3:28).

The Anger Problem

Haman was undoubtedly competent and adept at influencing others, enough to be appointed the king's right-hand man. He was also very cunning and dishonest, which allowed him to get close to the king and queen and influence other key nobles. Haman had a like-minded wife, Zeresh, who supported him and gave him advice. Further, Haman was not just any ordinary Persian. He was an Agagite—an enemy of Israel and Queen Esthers's people (Esther 3:10). He was not a man to trifle with. Still, Mordecai would not give ground to him.

Being disrespected by Mordecai was bad enough, but when he learned Mordecai was a Jew, he became livid! Haman's hatred was so great that he was going to exact revenge not on one but on all the Jews in the kingdom. It's one thing to scheme; it's another when hatred is involved. This wasn't just murdering one individual; this was planned genocide. There was no moral question in Haman's seared conscience. To him, he had every right to proceed on this despicable and deadly path to be paid in full with Jewish blood. But he was soon to learn that God indeed protects His children!

The Anger Response

Haman dupes the king into granting him his wish: the vile plot to destroy the Jews. There is no indication that the king had any hostility toward the Jews. However, the royal decree goes forth to annihilate the Jews, young and old (Esther 3:13). When Mordecai finds this out, he enlists Queen Esther to counter it. Queen Esther arranges for Haman to meet her and the king for a special banquet the next day. Taking this to mean he has found favor, Haman is puffed up with enormous pride and proceeds to boast about it.

At the same time, he is still bothered that Mordecai refuses to pay homage to him. He therefore seeks out counsel from those close to him. His wife and friends come up with a plan to get rid of Mordecai forever. They want Haman to build a pole seventy-five feet high and impale Mordecai on it for all to see (Esther 5). This is just the beginning of the events that will precede the Jews' demise. Naturally, nobody, especially a Jew, will cross the great Haman. But often in life, plans might not go as expected. Many times, they backfire and may come back to haunt a person. Strangely, before the banquet, something happens with the king.

The Anger Consequences

The king, possibly troubled with the earlier mandate to kill all Jews, can't sleep. He reviews the most recent history of his kingdom. In doing so, he discovers that Mordecai is the one who saved him, and desires to reward him. This is the same Mordecai who is under a virtual death sentence with the rest of his people. Afterward, devious Haman walks in to tell the king about hanging the same individual—Mordecai. But before Haman can speak, the king asks what reward should be given to someone who would delight the king. Of course, arrogant Haman thinks the king is talking about him. In response, he tells the king to place a magnificent robe on the honored person, put him on a horse, and have him led throughout the entire city for all to see that the king is bestowing favor upon him.

Thus, Haman's scheme to murder Mordecai, for the time being, is foiled by his own words. Not only is he not allowed to present his plan, but inadvertently he gives the king advice on how to honor someone else. And to his surprise, this someone turns out to be Mordecai. Rather than being dishonored and hung for all to see, he is to be celebrated. What a blow—this is the ultimate boomerang effect—it is not Haman but Mordecai who is to be honored. Ironically, the person leading him throughout the city is Haman. When he goes home, Haman is distraught, believing he is also falling out of favor, which may ruin his plan. However, at that very moment, he is summoned to attend Queen Esther's banquet that she has prepared for him and the King (Esther 6).

During the banquet, the king grants Queen Esther a favor. She asks that her people be saved from certain death. This is when the king finds out that she is a Jewess. Because of his love for her, he honors her. He then wants to know which man would do such a thing. She responds that the man is none other than Haman, sitting there with them. The king becomes so upset; he storms out. No doubt, Haman is shocked by who the queen really is. Knowing he is in trouble, Haman falls on the couch next to the queen to beg for his life.

But it gets worse for Haman—the king returns at that instant. Believing he is molesting his queen, King Xerxes seals Haman's fate when told about the pole built for Mordecai. Judgment is now rendered. Haman is taken out and impaled on the same pole he made for the person he hated so much (Esther 7). This all-consuming hatred he had for another has led to his death, with his entire family watching in horror from their home.

Subsequently, Mordecai is brought forth, and Queen Esther tells the king she is related to him. Mordecai is given Haman's position and estate. Further, the king allowed the Jews to protect themselves from any attack, since he could not undo the previous mandate. Later, instead of the Jews being destroyed, they fought back and were victorious (Esther 8). It is remembered today as the day of Purim (for the enemies had cast the *pur* [the lot] against them, and God saved them from being massacred). In a further twist to the story, Queen Esther made one more request that Haman's ten sons join him in the same type of death—by impaling (Esther 9). She knew that they would be a threat to the Jews if they remained.

In the end, Haman and his family, who schemed and plotted so much evil, were gone forever. Those they wanted to destroy lived on. Subsequently, Esther remained queen, and Mordecai remained at King Xerxes's right hand. He served both of them as an honest, valued, and trusted adviser (Esther 10). Thus, under God's continued protection, His people continued to live and be safe!

Hot Buttons

Haman had two prominent buttons: being **disrespected** and **intolerant** of the Jewish people. His anger came out when his deep-rooted hatred was triggered by a Jew, Mordecai, who happened to disrespect him. With enmity in his heart, he plotted to destroy not just one man but the entire Jewish race living there. In a twist of "fate," it destroyed him and his family.

Points to Ponder

Anger can lead to wicked schemes, plots, and plans. Haman is proof positive that some individuals can become angry and hate-filled. He lived for that hatred and wanted to take it out on others by making destructive plans targeting individuals and groups of people. As such, Haman was preoccupied and self-absorbed, spending a lot of time and energy plotting and scheming evil. Along these lines, he surrounded himself with like-minded folks who also became coconspirators. This included his wife, children, and others loyal to his cause.

Haman's acts were based on cold-blooded calculation and devious manipulation to accomplish his wickedness. Certainly, God condemns a person like this. In the end, all his plots backfired, for Mordecai and the Jews were spared. Haman and his family were defeated as God ensured that Haman's schemes were not only stopped, but used against him at every turn.

> In pride the wicked hotly pursue the afflicted; Let them be caught in the plots which they have devised. (Psalm 10:2 NASB)

Anger and hatred can lead to one's downfall. In Haman's case, he surrounded himself with those without wisdom, for they could not see the danger ahead and avert it. On that, wisdom and foolishness are the exact opposite. Wisdom and knowledge bless, while foolishness curses. Surrounded by fools, Haman took their foolish advice. Little did Haman realize that his plan would bring about his own destruction. After all, none were around to shout out the pitfalls and the demise he was headed toward—it was the blind leading the blind.

The words of the wicked lie in wait for blood, But the mouth of the upright will deliver them. The wicked are overthrown and are no more, But the house of the righteous will stand. (Proverbs 12:6–7 NASB)

God protects His own against angry and hate-filled people, especially those who do evil. How incredible is God, especially in times of attack, turmoil, or upheaval? God's plans will always outdo and outlast man's plans. First, God used Mordecai and Esther to do His will. In this case, Mordecai raised Esther and gave her godly counsel before and after she became queen. Then, by saving the king and finding favor with him, Mordecai and Esther would save their people, the Jews. Above all, they placed their faith in Him. In return, God protected them against all sorts of evil and ensured their deliverance from those who would do them harm. With his corrupt mind and vile actions, Haman devised his evil plans. Like many others throughout history, Haman wanted to vanquish the Jewish population. To this day, none have succeeded.

To be sure, God will save His people no matter where they are placed. Where else in history has a people been dispersed, prophesied to be brought together, and reunited in the Promised Land thousands of years later? Indeed, the Jewish people have settled in the area known today as the modern-day nation of Israel. It continues to survive and thrive, which is something that Haman and all haters of Israel would never have guessed would happen. And because God is God, His people will continue to prevail!

> *But as for you, O Jacob My servant, do not fear, Nor be dismayed, O Israel! For, see, I am going to save you from afar, And your descendants from the land of their captivity; And Jacob will return and be undisturbed And secure, with no one making him tremble.* (Jeremiah 46:27 NASB)

CHAPTER 8

A SERVANT'S UNFORGIVENESS

(Matthew 18)

---

*"But when that servant went out, he found one of
his fellow servants who owed him a hundred silver coins.
He grabbed him and began to choke him.
'Pay back what you owe me!' he demanded."*

(Matthew 18:28 NIV)

Context

This story is about an individual who exerts control over another, loses their temper, and then ends up as a violent attacker. But there is a twist here: this angry person had just received forgiveness! Yet even in this forgiven state, he refused to forgive others.

Since this book is about anger and angry people, it is also about our responses to them and how we should treat others with mercy and kindness, with forgiveness in our hearts (Ephesians 4:32). For this reason, we will look in-depth at personal forgiveness. We will also address God's forgiveness since we have been forgiven far more than we will ever forgive.

Here are some questions to keep in mind to gain greater insight on forgiveness:

1) Do I have a forgiving attitude?
2) Do I forgive fully, or do I hold a grudge?
3) How can I forgive from the heart when I can't forget what was done to me?
4) Why is forgiving sometimes so hard?
5) What are the consequences if I don't forgive?

Although this is a parable, it is timeless. It is a story we can all learn from and put into practice.

Biblical Background

Then Peter came to Jesus and asked, "Lord, how many times shall I forgive my brother or sister who sins against me? Up to seven times?" Jesus answered, "I tell you, not seven times, but seventy-seven times." (Matthew 18:21–22 NIV)

Peter approaches Jesus, wanting to know how often he should forgive. It appears Peter is either having an issue with a certain someone and is asking for some advice or is possibly looking to find favoritism with Jesus by acting bighearted. Peter offers up a forgiveness number meant to be much more than was expected. By saying seven times, he shows that he can go out of his way that many more times to overlook an offense. Ergo, Jesus should commend him.

Instead, surprising Peter, Jesus increases it elevenfold to seventy-seven times. This is a significantly higher number, to be sure. Indeed, is there some correct number for forgiving? If so, shouldn't it just be one time, if from the heart? Interestingly, the Old Testament has a high number, not for forgiving but for revenge.

Lamech said to his wives, "Adah and Zillah, Listen to my voice, You wives of Lamech, Give heed to my speech, For I have killed a man for wounding me; And a boy for striking me; If Cain is avenged sevenfold, then Lamech seventy-sevenfold." (Genesis 4:23–24 NASB)

Jesus is saying that there is no exact amount when it comes to forgiving. In that, there are no limits to forgiveness; it might even exceed seventy-seven times! Why? Because although forgiveness is often a one-time occurrence, it can also happen several times or more. We should be prepared to forgive as many times as is needed.

Forgiveness is a genuine act, showing true mercy and grace, letting go of the offense, and giving it over to God to handle. Just going through the motions and pretending to act compassionately may instead

allow bitterness to take root with all sorts of ongoing malice toward the offender. But honestly, the
offense will most likely only affect *you* if there is no
genuine forgiveness. In other words, *you* will be the
one to suffer!

The Story

*Therefore, the kingdom of heaven is like a king who
wanted to settle accounts with his servants. As he
began the settlement, a man who owed him ten
thousand bags of gold was brought to him. Since he
was not able to pay, the master ordered that he and
his wife and his children and all that he had be sold
to repay the debt.* (Matthew 18:23–25 NIV)

Jesus shows how much the servant owes to his master. If the servant fails to pay, it will have far-reaching
consequences. Doubtless, this debt was an extraordinary amount. This wasn't ten thousand pieces of
gold, but rather ten thousand bags, each filled with
gold. We are talking about many millions of dollars
in today's terms, if not in the billions. Who has that
lying around? Not many of us, including the servant
here, who owes the debt to his master. And now the
master wants payment.

Because he cannot pay such a significant sum, the
servant will lose family, possessions, income, and end
up in prison, all in one act. What a desperate plight
he and his family are in. For this reason, the servant

speaks up, looking for a way out, and begging for additional time. In truth, he will never have enough money to pay his debt. Really, where is he going to get this unbelievable sum?

Incredibly, the master forgives all. What a fantastic thing to happen! All that weight off this servant's shoulders, this is a fresh start for him and his family. Those who have been in debt, with sizable amounts such as a mortgage or car payment, know the relief felt when the debt is finally paid. Here, the unpayable is paid off. The slate is wiped clean because the sympathetic master desires to show compassion and mercy. By this, one would think the servant would have peace at last. But not so, as the following action proves.

The Anger Problem

Astonishingly, he finds a servant who owes him a hundred silver coins, chokes him, and demands he pay him back. We have here a forgiven servant one minute and in the next moment, this same person is on the verge of committing murder. Didn't he just get his way by having a tremendous debt removed, or did he get a case of selective amnesia? Forgiven and forgotten—that is precisely what the master did. Didn't the master show him love and generosity by the act of forgiveness? What is happening here? It appears this servant has no empathy or love, for if he did, he could easily forgive the debt, as the value of the bags of gold that he did not repay are worth much more than what he is owed—some silver coins, a significantly lesser amount.

On a personal note, I don't recall ever being choked, but I had a similar terrifying experience taking my last breath. While in the Navy and conducting water survival training with a parachute, we simulated ejecting out of an aircraft and landing in the ocean. I was harnessed up and walked off a high platform, falling into the swimming pool. Once in the water and with the parachute on top of me, I swam backward to find the edge. I went hand over hand till I was supposed to find it. Once located, with both hands, I was supposed to fling the parachute over my head and breathe. The problem is, I couldn't find the parachute edge.

Just about ready to run out of air, I thankfully found the edge. Throwing the parachute over my head, I gasped in the needed air. I looked up at the instructors on the platform for some sign of the danger I had been in. I saw none, for they were facing each other and deep in conversation. When I was running out of breath and focused on survival by any means, they were casually enjoying each other's company. There was no concern for my life. Was I upset? Yes, because I believed they would help me if it quickly became a life-and-death situation. I brought this example up because we often trust those who have our back or at least should have. For this reason, my sympathies here are with the servant who innocently trusted another and nearly lost his life. And yes, I forgave my instructors.

So then, shouldn't the forgiven servant have been more patient and forgiving? How should he have treated his fellow servant (neighbor)? Maybe we should heed what Jesus said about how we are to be.

> Jesus replied: "Love the Lord your God with all your heart and with all your soul and with all your mind." This is the first and greatest commandment. And the second is like it: "Love your neighbor as yourself." All the Law and the Prophets hang on these two commandments. (Matthew 22:37–40 NIV)

The Anger Response

The servant pleads the very same plea the angry servant did with the master. But the angry and forgiven servant refuses to forgive and then callously has the debtor thrown into prison. The borrower is not working and languishing there. Any hope of getting out, at least in the short term, is in doubt.

The forgiven servant mistakenly believes "justice" has been served. By using the legal system, he ends up punishing another. He is probably feeling good about himself as he and his family go about their lives and perhaps even celebrate the lifting of the debt burden. At the same time, his action has spread misery to another family. The imprisoned servant's family isn't celebrating anything; they are weeping at the injustice. Fortunately, others had seen what he did and told the master. Thankfully, true justice was soon to occur.

The Consequences

First, the forgiven servant is called "wicked." The mercy shown to him was the same mercy he should have demonstrated toward the other servant. Because he refuses to do so, the master deals harshly with him. Second, the servant is thrown in prison for his previous debt. The same legal system he abused has now been turned against him. His chance of ever getting out is zero. And third, to make his situation worse, he will be tortured—an awful end to this story. The lesson for us is clear: the Master (God) wants each of us to know how serious the act of forgiveness is, whether receiving it, giving it, or withholding it.

Hot Buttons

Indeed, the servant was focused on himself and worldly goods, especially money. He was in extreme debt, but it was forgiven. When the other servant didn't repay, his buttons of **forgiveness** and **empathy** (or lack thereof) were pushed. He was enraged, went ballistic, and nearly killed him. He was without love and mercy for another in need. In the end, he repaid the debt he owed—with his life.

Points to Ponder

Anger can consume! We need to consider "throttling back" and not act so hasty, especially if we become angry. As we have seen, anger can have devastating consequences. In this story, the servant quickly becomes angry, and overtaking him completely. He doesn't even take the time to talk before putting both hands around the other servant's neck to choke him. This can kill, right? The wicked servant is blinded with hatred—he cannot see beyond this moment of vengeance. Like Cain, sin has been crouching at his door and now springs into action, engulfing and consuming his life. Fortunately, he stops short of killing the other servant. And thankfully, others eventually come to the rescue.

> *Cease from anger and forsake wrath; Do not fret; it leads only to evildoing.* (Psalm 37:8 NASB)

Unlike the wicked servant who was faithless and would not forgive, our faith allows us to recognize this same forgiveness from God. We can show love, kindness, goodness, mercy, and forgiveness to others because the same has been shown to us by God.

God's anger is just and forgiving! To be sure, God can sometimes get angry; however, unlike the wicked servant, God's anger is slow, full of love, and forgiving.

*But you are a forgiving God, gracious and com-
passionate, slow to anger and abounding in love.*
(Nehemiah 9:17 NIV)

And because He is a just God, sin (though it may
be forgiven) is never tolerated! Fortunately, God
shows His grace and mercy most bountifully, especially when we do wrong and sin. He will often forgive
solely out of His kindness and compassion or when
someone repents (turns away from sin) and asks for
forgiveness. Again, He is a forgiving God!

*The Lord our God is merciful and forgiving, even though
we have rebelled against him;* (Daniel 9:9 NIV)

*Therefore the Lord longs to be gracious to you, And
therefore He waits on high to have compassion on
you. For the Lord is a God of justice; How blessed are
all those who long for Him.* (Isaiah 30:18 NASB)

Forgive and let go! Forgiveness is the act of letting go of a wrong or perceived wrong. We can be
released from any resentment, hatred, or bitterness
when this happens. As such, it helps to prevent an
act of revenge. Forgiveness also removes an anchor
around the neck, takes a weight off the shoulders,
and dismantles the walls that might surround us.
Furthermore, forgiveness is granting another a par-
don for what was done.

Is the wicked servant an isolated case? Unfortunately, because we live in a fallen world, hurtful words and actions are always happening. Many choose not to forgive, just as in the servant's time. The choice is ours— to go the way of this unforgiving world or to choose forgiveness and overlook all insults, acts, or other perceived or actual wrongs when they come. Like the wicked servant, unforgiveness has a way of making hearts hard and inflicting pain that causes suffering.

Unforgiveness destroys relationships, makes people bitter, and can negatively affect how one sees others and how they see you. No doubt, that's not the path we want to follow.

> *Be kind to one another, tender-hearted, forgiving each other, just as God in Christ also has forgiven you.* (Ephesians 4:32 NASB)

There is a caveat on forgiving. If we choose not to forgive others, God will not forgive us. Again, *we* will not be forgiven.

> *For if you forgive others for their transgressions, your heavenly Father will also forgive you. But if you do not forgive others, then your Father will not forgive your transgressions.* (Matthew 6:14–15 NASB)

God truly forgives, so let us do likewise. His forgiveness is divine; it is available for all who seek Him. When confession happens, He will cover the sin, and any guilt can be completely forgotten. Whatever sin there is, one is released from it. God has used many who were forgiven and then redeemed: Jacob (a liar), Moses (a murderer), David (an adulterer and murder), Zachariah (a cheater), Peter (a liar), Paul (a murderer), and the list goes on and on.

And their sins and their lawless deeds I will remember no more. (Hebrews 10:17 NASB)

Forgiveness and unforgiveness have consequences. One of the most significant effects of forgiveness is that God can help us with mercy and grace, especially in a broken relationship between two very close people. We are also asked to do our share of forgiving, especially if a possible restoration is to happen. If you have ever had a relationship broken and restored, there is much emotional outpouring of both parties' love. In the end, forgiving others allows us (and them) to become wiser and healthier, with a strengthened and revitalized relationship!

Does it always work out? Sadly, and painfully . . . no. Sometimes the other person might be unwilling to forgive, at least for the time being, and might even end up holding a grudge. Still, it doesn't mean we shouldn't try to do the right thing and pray for them while having good thoughts about them.

On the other hand, unforgiveness is a path littered with many regrets. Many adverse effects can occur, such as dwelling on the past, becoming a complainer, having a chip on the shoulder, or being less trusting. There might be an unhealthy fixation on revenge. None of the preceding is healthy—spiritually, mentally, emotionally, or physically.

> *See to it that no one comes short of the grace of God; that no root of bitterness springing up causes trouble, and by it many be defiled.* (Hebrews 12:15 NASB)

Forgiveness is hard sometimes! Many of us are not trying to be unforgiving, but forgiveness can be so very hard. There is no easy cookie-cutter solution to forgiveness; every person is different, and every situation is different. As a result, several issues might arise. To make matters more complicated, the other person might not want to communicate. Also, walls might go up (by you or them) to avoid being hurt again (don't prisons have walls).

Further, the timing might not be right; both people need to have their ears ready to listen to the other person. Avoiding the person might work in some cases and for some time. However, if the person is your spouse or neighbor or family member or boss or someone close, then what? And what if your hot button pushes their hot button? No doubt, things can get out of hand quickly.

Therefore, the critical question to ask is this: is your peace worth it to carry on and do battle, or is it time to let the past go and forgive from your heart? Perhaps you are being called to go forth and be the one to initiate forgiveness with a loved one, friend, or anyone else in need of God's love. Jesus said:

> *Blessed are the peacemakers, for they will be called children of God.* (Matthew 5:9 NIV)

Practice forgiveness DAILY. Forgive, forgive, forgive! To begin, make a list of people who have wronged you. Pray for each of these people. Forgive them from the heart. Now, give them over to God for Him to handle. Hopefully, this will begin the process of restoring a broken relationship. Please continue to have an attitude of forgiveness and treat them with kindness and respect. The rest is in God's hands. Sometimes, all of your efforts might seem to be in vain; the relationship is strained to the point where it doesn't look good for now. Don't be discouraged; remember God is going before you and working behind the scenes. And pray! The Holy Spirit is there to guide and provide comfort, so please be patient and watchful for divine intervention.

Again, we are called to forgive. It is not an option. It is for our benefit as well as the benefit of others. So have a forgiving disposition, forgive all, and do it from your heart with love and with no limit. God loves us and forgives all we have done, without limitation. Should we do less?

We have come to know and have believed the love which God has for us. God is love, and the one who abides in love abides in God, and God abides in him. (1 John 4:16 NASB)

CHAPTER 9

AN OLDER BROTHER'S RESENTMENT

(Luke 15)

"The older brother became angry and refused to go in. So his father went out and pleaded with him."

(Luke 15:28 NIV)

Context

Is sibling rivalry imagined or real? Likewise, does birth order make a difference? Does special treatment exist if one is the firstborn or the "baby?" In the Bible, this type of rivalry appears several times (Cain and Abel, Jacob and Esau, Joseph and his brothers, Leah and Rachel, Amnon and Absalom, and Absalom's brothers). Many of us, too, have grown up with siblings, perhaps experiencing what one would call somewhat challenging relationships. On one hand, this rivalry can result in friendly competition and closeness. On the other hand, at times, this competition might be heated and contentious.

To be sure, anger might come about for different reasons: envy, feeling put down, being left out, etc. It can end up in a real emotional tug-of-war with constant strife, miscommunication, arguments, fights, and even broken relationships. In this story, Jesus tells us about two brothers, one older and one younger. And though many of us are familiar with the younger "Prodigal" son's story, our focus will be on his older brother and his anger toward his brother and, surprisingly, toward his father.

Biblical Background

Jesus's ministry had been in full swing for about three years. As the Son of God, He was a spiritual leader, minister, healer, and miracle maker. He was called "rabbi" (religious teacher); thus, He would often meet with the multitude to instruct on spiritual lessons. One of the most effective tools Jesus used in His teaching was the parable, which was an illustration from everyday life to better explain and understand spiritual matters. At times, He would explain what appeared to have been hidden meaning. The story in the previous chapter was also a parable.

Even though the audience for these lessons was often the masses (the common folk), Jesus sometimes spoke in parables to the disciples and the Pharisees, a strict religious sect who considered themselves experts in the law and who would sometimes clash with Jesus over doctrine. Curiously, in this account, Jesus had been at a Pharisee's house for dinner, and later they were present in the crowds as He spoke. Nevertheless, the Pharisees weren't very pleased with what Jesus said.

Doubtless, the Pharisees would have heard this parable and similar ones on the same topic of being lost. It is the third in a series of three regarding being lost (the lost sheep, the lost coin, and the lost son) from the Gospel of Luke, Chapter 15. All three allude to a spiritually lost person who is subsequently found (and God rejoices!). Though this story starts out chiefly about the infamous lost "Prodigal Son" and his subsequent forgiveness, it is also about his older brother, who is stern and legalistic. We can see the blame game he fosters when his younger brother doesn't measure up to a certain standard (his, that is). As a result, the older brother becomes resentful and angry and holds a grudge, not unlike how the Pharisees viewed Jesus.

The Story

This story starts with a presumed wealthy landowner and his two sons overlooking a large estate. In those days, as was the custom, the older son typically received the most significant portion of the inheritance when the father passed away. The younger son was also entitled to a share, though a lesser amount. All the same, in the second son's case, it appears that youthful desires preempted any sense of duty. He no longer wanted to continue to work the estate but instead experience all that life had to offer—action, excitement, and desires to fulfill.

So, feeling that he deserved the money now, the young brother proceeded to ask his father for his inheritance, and surprisingly the father agreed. No doubt, this didn't sit well with the older brother since he probably believed his younger brother was shirking his duties, not sharing responsibilities for the estate, and possibly cutting into his inheritance as the oldest child.

Just like that, the younger brother headed off into the world and dove headfirst into wild living. At first, it appeared he had access to a seemingly endless amount of money. But soon enough, when the money ran out, his newfound (bought) friends abandoned him. This big spender and squanderer of wealth hit rock bottom very, very hard. He was bankrupt and without resources, and there was no one around to help him. From wealth to poverty, could it get any worse? Yes, because he ended up in one of the few places that would hire him—in a pig patch. Here, he was surrounded not by others of his kind, but by pigs.

Realizing he had done wrong and suffering in his present circumstances, he regretted throwing away the life he once had. He wanted to repent, confess all to his father, and get a second chance at life, even if it was as a lowly servant. Therefore, with a glimmer of hope, he headed out in the direction of home.

But while he was still a long way off, his father saw him and felt compassion for him, and ran and embraced him and kissed him. (Luke 15:20 NASB)

The father was full of emotion, showering much affection upon his son. He was happy his son was alive and now back with him; he did not condemn his actions but loved him! As a result of all he had been through, the son was repentant. He has learned a valuable lifelong lesson. The son was humble and no longer full of pride and cockiness; he was contrite.

The "Prodigal" son was indeed found, and the dead had been brought back to life; hence the father rejoiced! A party was then set up to celebrate the safe return and tell all that his lost son was alive and had returned. The entire household, save one (the older brother), went into action to prepare for this joyful event. Undoubtedly, any parent who has had a child in danger who comes through safely can feel great relief. They will often want to show others how thankful they are. On the other hand, the older brother's reaction was anything but glad, and unlike his father, he was not so grateful. He was angry!

The Anger Problem

The older brother was hot! Hadn't he remained and toiled on, doing everything expected of him? Surely, he had every right to be upset and bitter about what his younger brother did. In his hard-heartedness, rather than being thankful for his brother's safe return, the older brother chose to hold a grudge and not join in the festivities.

The Anger Response

The father is disappointed when he hears about his oldest son's decision. So he seeks him out with the desire to reunite the two brothers. In a complete huff, the older brother turns on his father, accusing him with point-by-point condemnation. Not only does he condemn his brother's actions, but also his father's "wrong" efforts as well. The older brother thinks the party is not fair. In fact, it is an injustice that he never got a party for doing right.

The Consequences

Gently and kindly, the father reaffirms his love for his oldest son and is also thankful his younger son has returned unharmed. He explains that celebrating with a banquet shows the joy of regaining one who was lost. The older son doesn't (or can't) understand because he, too, is lost. His heart has hardened because of unforgiveness. It isn't just a chip on his shoulder; he is now carrying a plank. Resentment can be a heavy burden. In the end, the father attempts to reason with him, but it is unclear if the older son is even listening. Without concern for his family, the oldest son is now living in a pig pen of his own making, wallowing in bitterness and resentfulness, and perhaps headed to his own demise.

Hot Buttons

The older brother's buttons were feeling **morally outraged, disrespected, and humiliated,** and to a lesser extent, **greedy and betrayed.** This ended in resentment and constant brooding, all ingredients for a hardened and unforgiving life.

Points to Ponder

Be careful in judging others! Is this a parable about an angry, upset older brother or something more? In truth, the older brother is the Pharisee, and the father is our Father God. This story is somewhat about religion and having the right relationship with God. Indeed, Jesus is calling out the Pharisees because they had a habit of calling out other sinners but ignored their own sins (Luke 18:9-14). It begs the question: isn't it better to forgive and rejoice at those who have returned to the fold and have been delivered from evil or, like the Pharisees, continue to judge them?

The older son needed saving too, and though he was physically alive, he was spiritually dead. Both the older son and Pharisees did everything by the Book, for they obeyed the law to the letter. However, if one were to break the law, they had a way out to "save" themselves. One could have sin absolved by going to the temple with an animal sacrifice. It was a physical act with a spiritual overtone. Though many people have tried to keep the law, only One has succeeded—Jesus.

Truly, one may have "religion," but if it is continuously disapproving, devoid of a personal relationship with God, and judgmental, it could lead to a joyless life traveling on an unholy path. In their resentment and unforgiveness, these same religious folks had reached their point of no return. In the end, they angrily wanted to get rid of Jesus because he wasn't toeing the party line to do what they had expected, which was to punish rather than forgive.

Now the Pharisees, who were lovers of money, were listening to all these things and were scoffing at Him. And He said to them, "You are those who justify yourselves in the sight of men, but God knows your hearts; for that which is highly esteemed among men is detestable in the sight of God." (Luke 16:14–17 NASB)

It is always better to overlook an offense. It is much wiser to overlook an offense than continue to hold on to one. Resentment can often lead to bitterness, eventually wearing a person down with emotional, mental, and physical issues. In the older brother's case, he became resentful after having a lot of time to think about the situation. Annoyed and agitated and biding his time, he held back his true feelings. He emptied both barrels at his father when the time presented itself, berating his father with great disrespect.

When we exalt ourselves, question decisions, and possibly even accuse, we presume we know better than those in authority. If one acts this way, those in authority have an easy solution: let us go. Thankfully, the father in this story does not.

So then, let us not be like the angry and ungrateful older brother but be thankful for our many blessings. Let us do our utmost not to complain, judge, grumble, be selfish, jealous, or arrogant. Instead, be content with a Father who watches over us. In doing so, we can and should trust Him in all matters relying on His wisdom and not ours, for our wisdom will always fall short. For this reason, it is wiser to *proclaim* (exalting and praising God) and not to *complain* (about those around us)!

Do not complain, brethren, against one another, so that you yourselves may not be judged; behold, the Judge is standing right at the door. (James 5:9 NASB)

Do everything without grumbling or arguing, so that you may become blameless and pure, "children of God" . . . (Philippians 2:14-15 NIV)

I will exalt you, my God the King; I will praise your name for ever and ever. Every day I will praise you and extol your name for ever and ever. (Psalm 145:1-3 NIV)

CHAPTER 10

PETER ACTING RASHLY

(John 18)

Then Simon Peter, who had a sword,
drew it and struck the high priest's servant,
cutting off his right ear.

(John 18:10 NIV)

Context

One of the greatest names in the Christian faith is Peter (also known as Simon). As one of the first followers chosen, and a devoted disciple for nearly three years, he was fiercely loyal to Jesus and was part of the inner circle with James and John. Together with Jesus, they traveled up and down Judea, ministering to the people. By being that close to Him, the disciples continually heard the gospel and saw firsthand how to live this new faith. Indeed, who better than Peter to practice loving others and being patient and peaceful?

Unfortunately, to the detriment of himself and others, he didn't always behave accordingly. The critical question is, why did he act contrary to what was taught?

Biblical Background

To start, Jesus chose this fisherman to cast his net over many people and lead the faithful. Although he spent much of his life in Galilee, on land and sea, Peter's impact would be felt worldwide. Peter might have appeared to be an "ordinary" man, but was not. He received substantial theological training up close and personal from Jesus, which later led to a practical hands-on ministry. Peter's writings in First and Second Peter are anything but a simple fisherman's account of life. They are deep and insightful wisdom written for Christians.

Living in Galilee, Peter would have been familiar with its religious leaders and elites. They were comprised of the high priest and priests and two other important religious groups called the Pharisees and the Sadducees. The Sanhedrin, the highest religious authority, consisted of the groups above. In addition, there were teachers and scribes to round out those with influence. Simultaneously, two rulers would have affected his life—the Jewish civil authority and the occupying Roman military rule. However, even among these religious leaders and "rulers," Peter was a man of deep conviction who understood that his one Ruler was God. Unlike the religious leaders,

Peter believed that Jesus was the Messiah, the Son of God. To them, this idea was blasphemy, the effects of which Peter would have witnessed.

Because of Peter's faith, Jesus chose him to be the "rock" (Petra) on which the early church would be built (Matthew 16:18). Peter, carrying out this mantle of responsibility, would lead many new believers in holy living. Still, this man of faith seems to be a paradox because he could sometimes be impatient and act rashly. So why would God choose him to become one of the first leaders of His church?

The Story

Therefore the chief priests and the Pharisees convened a council, and were saying, "What are we doing? For this man is performing many signs. If we let Him go on like this, all men will believe in Him, and the Romans will come and take away both our place and our nation." But one of them, Caiaphas, who was high priest that year, said to them, "You know nothing at all, nor do you take into account that it is expedient for you that one man die for the people, and that the whole nation not perish. (John 11:47–50 NASB)

Jesus, nearing the end of His ministry on earth, had just raised Lazarus from the dead in front of an amazed crowd. Many came to believe in Him, while others doubted. Some doubters were outright confused and went to see the Pharisees for an explanation

(John 11). After all, weren't they the experts in these matters? These learned people had eyewitness accounts and a good recollection of the miracles Jesus was purported to perform. They also experienced his teachings firsthand but would not accept them (more about this in the next chapter).

With no other options available in their evil minds, the decision was eventually made to end Jesus's life. Ironically, He was the very One, the Messiah, who they were waiting for as their savior and leader. Nevertheless, by doing this deed, they would get rid of Him once and for all, get their lives back, and all would soon be "normal" again. Thus, they plotted to falsely accuse Him and moved quickly to arrest Him, hoping He would be tried and receive the death sentence. However, in the wings was Peter, who was about to respond just as quickly.

The Anger Problem

With the arrest warrant issued, the conspirators had a willful participant to betray Him in their evil plot. Judas led the way to the Garden of Gethsemane where Jesus, Peter, James, and John were to be found. As the conspirators arrived in the garden, Jesus wasn't surprised that they had come. That is because He knew what was happening and what was going to happen. Jesus had predicted events earlier, and now they were about to take place to fulfill prophecy (Psalm 22, 118:22–24; Isaiah 52–53; Zechariah 12:10; Matthew 12:40, 16:4).

This night would not be a typical one. The arrest scene was an incredible one. Just as Jesus identified Himself, all the arresters fell to the ground. Judas kissed Jesus to confirm His identity, thereby affirming Judas's treachery. Peter stood by nervously, perhaps realizing that Jesus was soon to depart. He had to decide whether to act.

Earlier, Peter impulsively spoke out, contradicting Jesus on events that were to take place. Because of this, Jesus rebuked him (Matthew 16:21–23). He explained that Peter looked at man's concerns, not God's. Rather than listen to Jesus and let the "legal" process take place or choose any other peaceful course of action available, Peter was about to do something rash.

Why was Peter behaving this way and about to do something wrong? More to the point: why was Peter so different from the others? Why not just toe the line, follow in lockstep with the rest, and let events unfold as predicted? We know to some degree that he was quick to think (and act) because of his life at sea. But did this truly carry over to actions on land? And then again, perhaps he also might have had anger or self-control issues.

On the one hand, Peter's life on the Sea of Galilee was one of hard work in an ever-changing and sometimes fast-paced environment. Once underway, he would have had concerns about the weather, sea state, and maneuvering safely. In addition, he would have continually juggled multiple duties of locating the fish, casting nets, hauling in the catch, and returning to shore—all the while without losing equipment or human lives. This type of experience would lend itself to his continued survival.

On the other hand, it appears Peter might have possessed an "impulsive" personality. An example of this is when he and others were fishing far from land. The weather turned on them with high winds and high seas buffeting the boat. Then Jesus, out of nowhere, was walking toward them on water (Matthew 14:25). He called out to them not to be afraid, for they thought Jesus was a ghost. With little hesitation, Peter asked Jesus to call for him, which He did. Peter then stepped out of the boat and walked on water toward Jesus. Maybe Peter truly believed he would be safe because Jesus had calmed a storm earlier by rebuking it (Mark 4:39).

With an act of faith, Peter believed at first. He was walking on water, and what a success! But then Peter looked around and became afraid. When he did that, he started to sink. To keep from drowning, Peter shouted out to Jesus to save him, which He did (Matthew 14:28–31). For Peter, this was a test of faith that didn't exactly turn out too well. By acting impulsively, he put his life on the line, and his faith, forgetting that God was looking out for him all the time.

Now we might have a better picture to explain the "why" of Peter's behavior. As can be seen, he was both quick-thinking and impulsive. But there might be one other explanation of his behavior—fear. Could this feeling possibly have contributed to his actions in high-stress situations? In short, could fear have played a significant role in Peter's life, to the point of him either getting angry or losing control?

The Anger Response

Then Simon Peter, who had a sword, drew it and struck the high priest's servant, cutting off his right ear. (John 18:10 NIV)

Returning to the dimly lit garden where there was much confusion, Peter saw the impending demise of Jesus unfolding right before his eyes. But again, Jesus had warned all the disciples twice about what was about to happen. If anything was going to be done, they were to trust Jesus in what He told them and let the events play out. However, Peter thought that he could still prevent it from happening. He was going to do things his way and disregard Jesus's request. Turning the other cheek was not an option. Peter was armed and prepared to fight if necessary.

What were Peter's true intentions? Prove his loyalty to Jesus by possibly sacrificing his own life to the cause? Delay the arrest? Wound, maim, or perhaps kill another person who was just there to do their job? Hadn't Jesus taught about loving others? Yes, but Peter wasn't listening on this occasion because it appeared he was in a state of fear! Finally, unable or unwilling to control himself, Peter took out his sword and used it. In defending Jesus, he swung it and cut off the closest person's ear.

The Consequences

Jesus commanded Peter, "Put your sword away! Shall I not drink the cup the Father has given me?" (John 18:11 NIV)

With the foretold events coming true, Jesus was then arrested. But before He was taken away, Jesus reattached the servant's ear so it was wholly intact and working. All eyes were now on Peter. He was probably looked upon as a fool, or at least a hothead. Why should Peter not have done what he did?

1. He was attempting to preempt God, presupposing he knew better;
2. He could have gotten arrested and thrown in prison;
3. He could have been struck down and killed;
4. He jeopardized his fellow believers; and
5. Others possibly saw that he did not control himself, broke the law, and was not to be trusted.

I suspect all involved that night would have told others what happened, especially the servant whose ear was healed, Peter was blessed that he was not arrested. Had he been, his life would probably have ended with Jesus's. This is an abject lesson to be sure, for Jesus admonished Peter not to use violence, especially by the sword. Fortunately, Peter took it to heart, for there is no indication that he ever wielded the sword again. No doubt, because of the events that night and the ones to come, it must have been tough on Peter. All he knew was that Jesus was led away, and there wasn't much more he could do.

After Jesus's death, Peter understood what He prophesied. Jesus would be tried, convicted, and crucified, but would also rise again! In understanding that Jesus was doing His Father's will, Peter likewise would do God's will. With that probably at the forefront of his mind, he could confidently lead others based on what he had experienced and witnessed. And in defense of Peter, though we can view these events in hindsight, he had yet to experience them. In fact, there was still one more event to take place where Peter definitely "got" it.

On the day of Pentecost, and with the indwelling of God's Holy Spirit, Peter would be emboldened to step out in faith and encourage others to do the same as the early church grew (Acts 2). He must have occasionally looked back on events in his past and completely understood that God would get him through. By keeping his eyes on Jesus and placing his faith in Him, Peter was no longer afraid, impulsive, or apt to lose control, regardless of his surroundings. He was stepping out in faith, a real fisher of people, casting his net wide for many to believe just as he did.

Hot Buttons

Was Peter a hothead with uncontrolled impulses or just given into fear? Perhaps he was both based on the situation presented before him. His buttons were most likely **impatience, impulsiveness**, and **fear** of the unknown with **loss of control**. Given those buttons, he acted rashly and badly at times. But later, filled with the Holy Spirit, he was able to step out in faith and act responsibly and befitting of one who was a great church leader.

Points to Ponder

Do not repay evil with evil! How are we to act if we are offended by someone's actions or speech? Shouldn't we overlook the offense and turn the other cheek? The answer should be an emphatic yes. After all, most people don't go out of their way to perpetrate evil for no reason. There may be extenuating circumstances. The point is we don't know the why or what is going on with the other person.

If one opts for a payback instead of letting it go, this "revenge" is not justice, however much rationalized. No doubt, things can get out of hand very quickly, especially in one situation most of us share—driving.

Let's be honest; this is probably the most dangerous situation you can put yourself in, with high-speed and heavy weighing machines. A car can quickly turn into a deadly weapon in seconds. As an example, what do you do if another car cuts you off? Should you let them go by and get out of their way?

I say yes, you should overlook it. More times than not, many of these people are late and in a hurry. Now, you may argue that the driver deserves to be held responsible for their actions, particularly if they are endangering others and driving recklessly. Yes, they should be held accountable by the authorities. The police exist to sanction these lawbreakers, and eventually, they will get caught. There are peaceful options, including calling 911 and making a report, praying for them, and even blessing them (Romans 12:14).

Engaging in road rage only results in two hotheads in a heated duel. So please let it go! The goal is to de-escalate the situation and stay safe. To be sure, God will take care of the other person (the one breaking the law), no matter what they have done to you or me, whether driving or in another situation, that calls for us to keep our cool.

How might we learn from Peter and the events of that night in the garden? Undoubtedly, it was a precarious and dangerous situation. He instigated and then committed a violent act by taking his sword and using it. Fortunately for Peter, Jesus was right there to keep the peace. As a result, Peter was neither arrested nor struck down himself. He later understood that the better path was to control himself and overlook an offense.

We need to remember that God is indeed with us. This is true at all other times in our life, whether the danger is near or far. Therefore, be at peace, and be at rest in Him. Do not repay evil with evil, but with a blessing. Peter later wrote:

> *Do not repay evil with evil or insult with insult. On the contrary, repay evil with blessing, because to this you were called so that you may inherit a blessing. For "Whoever would love life and see good days must keep their tongue from evil and their lips from deceitful speech. They must turn from evil and do good; they must seek peace and pursue it."* (1 Peter 3:9–11 NIV)

Practice self-control in all situations. Peter not only turned out to be a student of self-control but he also ended up teaching it. In the New Testament, he would write that self-control was one of several essential items to grow one's faith (2 Peter 1:6). Peter must have recognized that he made impetuous and rash decisions in his earlier life, leading to foolish acts. Taking a lesson from Peter, practicing self-control can help us avoid making unwise and possibly costly decisions. Sadly, some decisions may never be reversed. By not practicing self-control, poor choices can lead to poor outcomes.

Unless it is a life-or-death situation, most decisions don't have to be made immediately. It might be wiser to sleep on it when your mind is synthesizing information (dreaming, that is). Waking up refreshed could lead to examining other alternatives not previously considered. In essence, going through this self-disciplined process could allow for making the best decision. Further, there is a connection to our faith. By exercising self-control and other godly qualities, we grow in our faith. Peter wrote:

> *For this very reason, make every effort to add to your faith goodness; and to goodness, knowledge; and to knowledge, self-control; and to self-control, perseverance; and to perseverance, godliness; and to godliness, mutual affection; and to mutual affection, love. For if you possess these qualities in increasing measure, they will keep you from being ineffective and unproductive in your knowledge of our Lord Jesus Christ.* (2 Peter 1:5–8 NIV)

Put your fear in the right place. Peter, at times, was afraid, which contributed to him acting spontaneously and recklessly. Two previous examples discussed included walking on water and in the garden. A third time was after the arrest of Jesus when Peter was waiting to see what would happen next. Finally, outside the courtyard, a woman pointed out that he was a follower of Jesus. As Peter was just about ready to be exposed, he denied the accusation as the rooster cried out (Matthew 26:69–75). When the Holy Spirit came to earth to indwell believers, Peter became a changed man and never lived in fear again. And since we have the same Holy Spirit, neither should we (Romans 8:15).

Fear can be very harmful and certainly cloud our judgment. Prolonged fear can undoubtedly be detrimental and lead to all sorts of mental, emotional, and physical problems or issues if not resolved. And with too much fear, one can be overwhelmed to the point of debilitation. In that event, one may shut down altogether. For these reasons, we are told not to fear but instead look to God, not on what is happening around us. Therefore, do not be afraid, but pray through all situations and ask for God's protection and strength.

Fear not, for I am with you; Be not dismayed, for I am your God. I will strengthen you, Yes, I will help you, I will uphold you with My righteous right hand. (Isaiah 41:10 NKJV)

In the end, Peter was an expert on fear and later concluded that the one fear we should possess is to fear God alone. It is a reverent and holy fear that honors God, the Almighty (1 Peter 2:17–20). When doing so, like Peter, we will surely be aware of all He has done and will do for us, now and always.

Trust God in all things. The central question is, where did Peter place his trust—God or himself? Earlier, while walking on water, Peter took his eyes off God and looked at his surroundings, and he began to sink. That night in the garden, as he was looking around and believing the situation was only going to get worse, Peter confidently took matters into his own hands. Eventually, this self-confidence was replaced with God-confidence. Looking back at that time in the garden, Peter understood that Jesus always had the situation well under control—it never warranted his act of "bravery."

With the Holy Spirit came a different, eternal perspective on life. As such, Peter stepped out in faith, energized and truly trusting in God. Likewise, we need to trust God in all things and move forward and upward till the day we are with Him forever. As Peter wrote:

> Blessed be the God and Father of our Lord Jesus Christ, who according to His great mercy has caused us to be born again to a living hope through the resurrection of Jesus Christ from the dead, to obtain an inheritance which is imperishable and undefiled and will not fade away, reserved in heaven for you. (1 Peter 1:3–4 NASB)

CHAPTER 11

PAUL AND HATRED'S BLINDNESS

(Acts 7–9)

But they cried out with a loud voice, and covered
their ears and rushed at him with one impulse.
When they had driven him out of the city,
they began stoning him; and the witnesses laid
aside their robes at the feet of a young man named Saul.

(Acts 7:57–58 NASB)

Context

Paul, like Peter, was a man of great faith. However, their backgrounds were worlds apart. You can call him Saul, Paul, Saint Paul, the transformed one, or the other half of the Peter and Paul team. His life story starts full of religiosity and on a mission full of hate. Nevertheless, it ends in a relationship with God and on a mission full of love. How is it that this "true" believer and follower of the law would one day walk away from what the Pharisees stood for? In fact, the change to Paul's life was incredible and unique. So who was Paul, what type of world did he live in, and how did his transformation occur?

Biblical Background

To begin, Paul was born both a Jew and, just as importantly, a Roman citizen (Acts 16:37). At first, he became a learned scholar dedicated to the Pharisees' cause. However, after his transformation as a believer in Jesus, his religious upbringing and Roman status proved instrumental in touching many with the gospel message of love and salvation. But before that happened, Paul only knew of life in a ruthless world under Roman rule. For the most part, it was devoid of love of neighbor, much less God.

It was a black and white world, with Rome as conqueror and ruler, wielding total power over many. Fear and intimidation were always in play. Rome sought absolute obedience over many across the globe, including Judea. Those in authority often used heavy-handed methods, including arrest, torture, and death by crucifixion. In Jesus's case, He received all three (Matthew 27:1–54).

In Judea, the people would be reminded daily of this hold on them, with a constant state of scrutiny. The people could see Roman soldiers on sentry duty and the king's soldiers possibly walking among the crowds. Also, the religious leaders would shuffle to and from the temple to instruct the faithful. All three played their respective roles in lording over the people. But they were not equivalent. The king and the religious leaders had Rome to follow.

Previously, the religious leaders had the Romans do their bidding and crucify Jesus, making sure He was gone and never to be returned (Matthew 27:57-66). They knew this to be accurate even as they probably heard of sightings and rumors that He was still alive (John 20:16, 19, 21:1). To them, these were just stories to be discounted and explained away. Since Jesus was now gone, couldn't they expect the followers of the "Way" (Acts 9:2) to desert the cause? And if Jesus, the "Messiah," was gone, how could He possibly help them now?

What they didn't count on was the "Good News" message resonating with many and the Holy Spirit appearing on the day of Pentecost, ten days after Jesus ascended into heaven (Acts 1:9). The Holy Spirit was indwelling these new believers. Slowly but surely, the church grew despite the opposition.

What especially troubled the religious leaders was this "Messiah" claim by others (John 4:25–26, 11:25–27; Luke 4:17–21; Matthew 16:16, 26:63–64). They didn't believe it was true, so how could others? To them, the Messiah had not yet come. However, these new followers of Jesus believed otherwise. The "Good News" message of repentance, forgiveness, and salvation took hold, placing the religious leaders' authority in doubt. This was a significant concern because it affected who and where to worship, provide offerings, and pray. It directly affected the temple's activities. Animal sacrifices had become a significant way of life for those desiring forgiveness and a steady source of income for many.

At the temple, an offender could pay for an animal substitute to remove their sin. A priest would then transfer the sin from the person onto the animal and sacrifice it. The shed blood covered over the offender's sin, and forgiveness was received. This had been the practice for centuries, beginning with Moses and handed down over the generations (Leviticus 4:27–35). But it was about to end.

There was a connection between the sacrificial system and Jesus. Being the "Lamb of God," He had sin placed upon Him by the Father (2 Corinthians 5:21; 1 Peter 2:24). Jesus willingly shed His blood for He who knew no sin became sin for us (1 Corinthians 5:21), thereby becoming a sacrificial atonement for the sin of all (Romans 3:25). John wrote:

> *The next day he saw Jesus coming to him and said, "Behold, the Lamb of God who takes away the sin of the world!"* (John 1:29 NASB)

To add more contempt from the Pharisees, Jesus spoke of a destroyed temple rising again:

Jesus answered them, "Destroy this temple, and in three days I will raise it up." (John 2:19 NASB)

Indeed, He was talking about Himself. The temple in Jerusalem was to be replaced. It would no longer be a physical building or specific locale. Instead, it would become individual temples (our bodies), wherein the Holy Spirit would reside.

Do you not know that you are a temple of God and that the Spirit of God dwells in you? (1 Corinthians 3:16 NASB)

Decades later, the Romans destroyed the rebuilt temple in Jerusalem, leaving only parts of the western wall standing. With this destruction, the religious leaders' power diminished. The Christian faith flourished more and more throughout the Roman Empire. The gospel message went forth to many Roman cities and Roman citizens, soldiers, those enslaved, and others. Yet, before the "Way" was to take hold, the religious leaders and Pharisees were to push back menacingly at this new flock.

The Story

And on that day a great persecution began against the church in Jerusalem, and they were all scattered throughout the regions of Judea and Samaria, except the apostles. Some devout men buried Stephen, and

*made loud lamentation over him. But Saul began
ravaging the church, entering house after house, and
dragging off men and women, he would put them in
prison.* (Acts 8:1–3 NASB)

To the religious leaders and Pharisees, getting rid of
Jesus wasn't good enough. It was now time to get rid
of His memory and His followers to stop the move-
ment's momentum before it could get too big. And so,
the persecution began. One Pharisee, Paul, became a
willing participant and led the charge. As he would
later describe himself:

*. . . a Hebrew of Hebrews; as to the Law, a Pharisee;
as to zeal, a persecutor of the church; as to the righteousness which is in the Law, found blameless.*
(Philippians 3:5–6 NASB)

At the time, there appeared to be Rome's tacit approval
for the Pharisees to seek out these believers whenever
needed and wherever found. Therefore, the Pharisees
and other like-minded haters began their intimidation. This was followed by beatings and then murder,
with Stephen as the first recorded martyr and Paul
in attendance (Acts 7:57–60). Mob action started to
rule the day; collective group thinking led to group
action that set into motion the persecution of the early
believers. The hunt was now in full swing to get rid of
them, once and for all. That is why Paul, full of malev-
olence, joined others to round up as many of these
converts as they could find.

The Anger Problem

Now Saul, still breathing threats and murder against the disciples of the Lord, went to the high priest. (Acts 9:1 NASB)

As one of the designated leaders, Paul gave heart and soul to the cause, learning and living its specific religious teachings and the Mosaic Law. However, those in power went one step further. They rendered the interpretation of the law and taught it at the synagogues, thereby influencing and controlling the Jewish population. Jesus spoke to this:

These people honor me with their lips, but their hearts are far from me. They worship me in vain; their teachings are merely human rules. (Matthew 15:8–9 NIV)

Many of these laws were targeted at physical effort on the Sabbath, which could be considered work. Rather than make life easier, this complicated life even more. They then added more rules to obey (and break), especially regarding the Sabbath (Matthew 12:1-8). With more laws came the possibility of more sinning and more reason to head to the temple to offer a sacrifice to receive forgiveness. Of course, this sacrifice wasn't free. It came at a price, meaning those who could afford it would "buy" their way out of sin.

To ensure the status quo wasn't interrupted, these condemning religious leaders executed plans to destroy all their "enemies." Spearheaded by Paul, he assured the continued control of the Jewish populace while attempting to end Jesus's legacy. With hate on his mind and murder in his heart, he acted relentlessly to destroy these fellow Jews who had become "blasphemers." But who really were these people he was set against?

Paul's knowledge about Jesus and His followers would have been narrow and biased, coming from the religious teachers and his circle of peers. He got caught up in institutionalized prejudice and discrimination. Paul wasn't about to sit down and reason with them. In his mind, he believed he was right, and they were wrong! Even if Paul had any intellectual curiosity about who Jesus truly was and what His followers believed, it was left at Paul's feet when Stephen was being stoned to death and forgave Paul and others. His hatred for Stephen and the other believers made him blind and deaf to the truth.

Paul believed he had all the answers. Hadn't he studied diligently and understood the workings of the law? Paul understood that obedience would be rewarded and disobedience would be punished. The message of the Messiah wasn't new to him. But Jesus as Savior, with whom he could have a personal relationship, was foreign to him. The God Paul knew was more distant and impersonal. After all, he believed he was doing God's work.

Calling Paul a zealot would be an understatement. Fanatics can be motivated by many issues, including religion. Their central aim can be to deny other beliefs (and remove those who won't agree with them), with the prime motivator of serving their deity. As a result, they end up with hardened hearts. Full of hatred and uncaring toward others, they seek and destroy. Paul was bent on completing this mission one hundred percent.

The Anger Response

He went to the high priest and asked him for letters to the synagogues in Damascus, so that if he found any there who belonged to the Way, whether men or women, he might take them as prisoners to Jerusalem. (Acts 9:1–2 NIV)

Not unlike the Roman soldiers, Paul and his companions could be brutal. These loyal "soldiers" made persecution an art form to make others suffer. Using intimidation, fear, physical abuse, beatings, arrest, trial, torture, and eventually crucifixion, they could achieve their objective of wiping out their opposition.

Paul, casting the net ever wider to find other believers wherever they were, pressed on to undo the work of many (including Peter, who spread his net to save, not destroy). Filled with blinding hatred on this mission of destruction, Paul pushed ahead to increase the numbers of those persecuted even higher. But on the way, his life was to take an unforeseen path.

The Consequences

As he was traveling, it happened that he was approaching Damascus, and suddenly a light from heaven flashed around him; and he fell to the ground and heard a voice saying to him, "Saul, Saul, why are you persecuting Me?" And he said, "Who are You, Lord?" And He said, "I am Jesus whom you are persecuting, but get up and enter the city, and it will be told you what you must do." (Acts 9:3–6 NASB)

This brilliant light left Paul blinded as he encountered this meeting with Jesus. Those with him eventually got him to their destination. But how could they help him any further, unsure if he would regain his sight? There was no Pharisee playbook for this. Fortunately for Paul, God sent a believer, Ananias, who agreed to care for Paul in his vulnerable state, despite Paul's hostile reputation.

Like Paul, so much of what we do and know about the physical world around us depends on what we see. This situation here can be very troubling and challenging, losing one of your senses, if not your key sense. Admittedly, if you have ever had trouble with your eyes, you might become fearful. Perhaps you have developed an eye disease, suffered a blood vessel break, needed to flush out irritants, or encountered an accident that directly affected your vision. I have experienced all of them, and any of them can make you feel helpless. At these times, God can also open our spiritual eyes, and with our focus on Him, we can lean on His strength to get us through.

> *So Ananias departed and entered the house, and after laying his hands on him said, "Brother Saul, the Lord Jesus, who appeared to you on the road by which you were coming, has sent me so that you may regain your sight and be filled with the Holy Spirit." And immediately there fell from his eyes something like scales, and he regained his sight, and he got up and was baptized; and he took food and was strengthened.* (Acts 9:17–19 NASB)

Considering all the carnage left by Paul, why would God use a man who hated Him to spread His Word and gain believers? The answer is that he didn't hate God; Paul believed in God. To be sure, he considered his mission to be just and righteous in destroying the new believers in Jesus, but that was not what God desired. Thus, Jesus asked: "Why are you persecuting Me?" Before Ananias arrived, this precise question must have perplexed Paul to no end while blind and in unfamiliar surroundings. Perhaps it allowed him to think and meditate about what was real, what he believed in, and if he would continue to hate and destroy others. With his faith in question and his life on pause, he must have considered his actions, especially what the law really meant.

In very little time, the "road to Damascus" experience drastically changed Paul's life and mission. When Ananias showed up, he would regain his vision (physically and spiritually) and become a new believer and be a significant part of the church he had persecuted. With a willing heart and the Holy Spirit, for the first time, he knew the truth. He believed that Jesus was who He said He was—the Son of God, the Messiah, and the Savior. Paul then traded in the Pharisees' hate for Jesus's love. This transformed him from a Christ-hater to a Christ-follower and leader. Thus, God would use Paul tremendously as one of Christianity's greatest advocates because Jesus further stated:

> But the Lord said to him, "Go, for he is a chosen instrument of Mine, to bear My name before the Gentiles and kings and the sons of Israel; for I will show him how much he must suffer for My name's sake." (Acts 9:15–16 NASB)

As a possible direct consequence, perhaps in no small measure for all the terrible things he had done earlier in his life to others, Paul did have a lifetime of suffering with many near-death situations (2 Corinthians 11:23–27).

Indeed, Paul's life was completely altered because he met Jesus. He became a new creation in Christ and now had a personal relationship with Him. Although he would have known of the God that met annually with the High Priest in the temple to atone for the nation, this was different. Paul found God was not callous, disinterested, or hard-hearted like the religious leaders and Pharisees who "represented" Him. Instead, there was a God who loved, cared for, and who reached out to him as He does with us. And like Paul, one can expect to face challenges and adversity when living a faith-based Christian life and spreading the same message of the Good News.

Paul is considered the Great Missionary, visiting many cities throughout the Roman Empire, encouraging the new churches there, and preaching the Good News. All the while, he was writing letters (the Epistles) providing instruction on the Christian life. His legacy began full of hate, immersed in religiosity, and ended full of love for others, and fully engaged in a one-on-one relationship with Jesus.

Hot Buttons

Paul was brainwashed into living a life of hate-filled religious dogma, where loving others was not part of it. His buttons were **intolerance, resentment, defending his "truth," and not ever being wrong**. Immersed in his belief system, he was right, and the new converts were wrong. Eventually, Paul found he was wrong, and they were right. He then spent the rest of his life living, loving, and preaching as much.

Points to Ponder

Hate can destroy your life. Hatred consumed Paul and was the life force that drove him and others into this murderous endeavor. Like Paul, if consumed with hate, one may have a narrowly focused and biased view of life, causing an inability to see and know the truth. Paul didn't realize he was also in the process of destroying himself. Hatred often consumes the hater. Had Paul not seen the "light," this most probably would have been his fate.

For those people full of hate, it can be unfortunate. They can become blind and deaf to others, often refusing to listen to those of a different mindset. These haters may attempt to hurt others through actions and speech, with words cutting as deeply as a knife. Paul carried this to an extreme. He killed people and destroyed families and their communities. He didn't bother to understand them because they were different. They loved and he hated. After his complete reversal, Paul teaches us to answer hate with love. Paul wrote:

> *Love does no wrong to a neighbor; therefore love is the fulfillment of the law.* (Romans 13:10 NASB).

Be careful who you follow. Like the Pharisees, many claim to represent God, but they represent either themselves or others plotting to do harm. As opposed to God (the Good Shepherd), they are black sheep attempting to take leadership and often are success-ful. They are themselves blind, leading others who are blind over a cliff to destruction.

Please be aware, take heed, and know who you're deal-ing with. There is only one true God. Paul found this out, and so can you. One way you can tell if your leader is on the right path is to answer the following questions:

1. Does their behavior (lifestyle) agree with the Bible?
2. Do they teach from the Bible?
3. Who are they aligned with doctrinally?

God does not contradict Himself, so if any counsel goes against God's Word, then you should reject it. Be discerning, keep your spiritual eyes wide open, and test all spirits with the Holy Spirit to see you safely through.

> *Beloved, do not believe every spirit, but test the spirits to see whether they are from God, because many false prophets have gone out into the world.* (1 John 4:1 NASB)

When you come to a fork in the road, choose wisely. Paul had free will and we have free will. At Damascus, when given a choice to continue on the road of hate, Paul wisely decided to follow the one of love and peace. Recall some forks in the road that we have pre-viously discussed, whereby people chose either good or evil. Once a choice was made, there was no turning back. We can look at the choices of Cain, Saul, Haman, and the unforgiving servant and see destructive consequences. God allowed many of these stories in the Bible as examples for us to learn from.

When we are confronted with a fork in the road, it is always wise to seek other godly folks and their counsel, study the Bible, and pray. And above all, seek the Holy Spirit for guidance and direction. As a special note, I always sleep on every vital life decision I must make. Although I try to look at all sides of the issue at hand and consider any consequences before I make a final decision, my mind is finite. Therefore, I seek God's will through the Holy Spirit by continuing to pray about it. In doing this, you and I are in the best possible position to make the right decision, usually confirmed with peace to follow. Paul wrote:

> *For this reason also, since the day we heard of it, we have not ceased to pray for you and to ask that you may be filled with the knowledge of His will in all spiritual wisdom and understanding.* (Colossians 1:9 NASB)

Having relationships means loving others. Paul was undoubtedly impacted by what he had done to the early believers. It must have weighed heavily on him for the rest of his life. After oppressing so many, Paul gained much insight into treating others with love. Truly transformed, he would have touched many kindly, gently, and patiently.

With a softened heart and the Holy Spirit's guiding presence, Paul was no longer someone who hated others. He loved them. Paul affirmed that this should be our aim too by writing:

And now these three remain: faith, hope and love. But the greatest of these is love. (1 Corinthians 13:13 NIV)

SECTION THREE

THE ANGER
SOLUTION

CHAPTER 12

CHOOSING WISELY

(Proverbs)

My son, do not forget my teaching,
But let your heart keep my commandments;
For length of days and years of life
And peace they will add to you.

(Proverbs 3:1–2 NASB)

Biblical Background

The book of Proverbs is a compilation of wise sayings broken down into thirty-one sections. These sayings can significantly help in many areas of life (including those with self-control and anger issues). This book is primarily behavior-oriented with consequences. In other words, the wrong action equals the wrong results, and the right action equals the right results. Since most of us want to do the right thing, the godly wisdom found in the book of Proverbs allows us to take it to heart to do things the right way.

By reading, meditating, and heeding the book of Proverbs, one can receive many benefits such as knowledge, understanding, blessing, favor, success, victory, protection, safety, health, peace, restful sleep, honor, a good name, and long life.

The Anger Solution

As we shall see, the book of Proverbs certainly has much to say about anger, especially when it leads to hate and wickedness. The subject of anger is addressed by unwise acts or other foolish behavior, which can lead to impatience and cause strife and temperament issues. Though it points out other failings or lack of proper behavior, the book of Proverbs also offers solutions for preventing future harmful actions.

There are unquestionably many other places where one can find wisdom, whether from advisers, mentors, family members, friends, or personal experience. We may also see "worldly" wisdom from many cultures, philosophers, and other thinkers. Worldly wisdom is based on sophisticated expertise and tries to make sense of human nature. It then offers the wisest choices on how to best interact with others or in a given situation. This wisdom is meant for us to do better, keep from doing wrong, and stay out of harm's way.

In this case, God's wisdom inspired the writing in the book of Proverbs, which makes it different from all other worldly wisdom. These wise sayings, primarily simple and to the point, are from people who had faith in God and were used by God (Solomon, Agur, and Lemuel). They were undoubtedly written to help us manage our anger, among other things. And because many other issues are addressed in the book of Proverbs, I recommend a word search in Proverbs for further insight, direction, and counsel.

So, please be mindful of the warnings in the book of Proverbs and not turn to foolish ways by making poor choices, including losing control and getting angry. Additionally, please avoid confrontations, quarrels, and fights; instead, remain calm, be patient with others, and be at peace with yourself. Last, pay careful attention to any path that might tempt you and lead you astray. Instead, seek God's wisdom, apply it, and be blessed!

Points to Ponder

A fool's way leads to many problems. Folly is the opposite of wisdom, for it lacks discernment or understanding. Fools will choose a path that will only be more problematic. A situation often worsens because there is a lack of awareness of what might occur next. As the circumstances deteriorate, fools become annoyed when things don't go their way. When this happens, they are apt to become confrontational. Losing their temper, they can get out of control and lash out, mocking and scoffing to justify their

wrong choice(s), which can lead directly to inappropriate behavior.

*Fools show their annoyance at once, but the prudent
overlook an insult.* (Proverbs 12:16 NIV)

**A hot-tempered person can end up in all kinds of
trouble.** Have you ever noticed how quickly someone
can emotionally light up over the slightest irritation? You don't want to be this type of person. A person with a short fuse is almost always ready to show
anger. There is little to hold them back, and they
often end up in confrontations and possibly doing
much harm to themselves and others. So what to do?
Pray, pray, and pray some more for them. Read the
book of Proverbs for insight and wisdom. Seek the
Holy Spirit's guidance and seek out other godly folks
(pastors, counselors, etc.) for advice.

*A quick-tempered person does foolish things,
and the one who devises evil schemes is hated.*
(Proverbs 14:17 NIV)

Wickedness and anger often go hand in hand. Many
evildoers (like Haman) meticulously plan to carry
out all sorts of wicked schemes in order to dictate,
enslave, or destroy others. They will spare no devious
act to carry out their plans, and if in power, will get
others to go along with them. But be assured, they
will end up failing and not get their way because, in
the end, God's justice will prevail.

Although these evildoers are "clever" at setting traps for others and baiting them, little do they realize they are the ones being snared. When the web fails, they often get furious, even to the point of insanity. Next, they will do anything to get out of the situation. This could mean abandoning or blaming others since their conscience has probably already been seared. And rather than face justice, they will continue on a path of self-destruction. Ultimately, no matter how long it takes, God protects the ones targeted and removes those doing the targeting.

> *The desire of the righteous is only good, But the expectation of the wicked is wrath.* (Proverbs 11:23 NASB)

Poor choices can lead to anger and harmful consequences. One poor choice is adultery. It can make the innocent spouse very angry. This breaking of marital vows is awful, not only for the other person but also because it breaks a covenant with God. Adultery never ends well. When found out, the injured partner's wrath can become great. The strife it can cause will be felt by all friends and family around the couple (especially their children). Another poor choice is jealousy, where emotions can run high and cause someone to feel ignored, confused, slighted, angry, or betrayed, especially if the actions are flagrant and hurtful. In both cases, there is usually deep pain for all involved and, most likely, harmful consequences to follow.

*But a man who commits adultery has no sense; who-
ever does so destroys himself. Blows and disgrace are
his lot, and his shame will never be wiped away. For
jealousy arouses a husband's fury, and he will show
no mercy when he takes revenge. He will not accept
any compensation; he will refuse a bribe, however
great it is.* (Proverbs 6:32–35 NIV)

Avoid quarrels; they only lead to strife! Like many,
I seek to avoid confrontations. But sometimes they
happen, and often very quickly. Before you know it,
it seems that you are in the presence of an aggressive, highly contentious person, regardless of fault.
It could happen anywhere and by anyone as you go
about your day-to-day life. So what can you do?

Here is some helpful guidance to avoid a possible
confrontational situation:

- Don't speak nonsense (Proverbs 10:8).
- Mind your own business (Proverbs 26:17).
- Don't overstay your welcome (Proverbs 25:17).
- Don't gossip (Proverbs 26:20).
- Don't mock (Proverbs 9:8).
- Above all else, show love to all, particularly
  when YOU are wronged (Proverbs 10:12).

Be patient and stay calm! One of the best solutions for
an angry person (you included) is being patient and
calm. You can show genuine kindness when you are

clear-minded, controlled, not heated, and no longer quick to do battle yourself. Hopefully, the angry person can begin to think more rationally and less emotionally. Indeed, showing patience with true humility can fill the situation with calm and turn the hothead into a cool head.

Better a patient person than a warrior, one with self-control than one who takes a city. (Proverbs 16:32 NIV)

Exercise diplomacy! Christians are called to be God's ambassadors. This means to behave respectfully, courteously, and thoughtfully toward others, not in some situations but in all situations. How we live in this world and treat others reflects directly on our beliefs, motivations, and core values. We must be authentic representatives of Christ, receiving godly wisdom from the Holy Spirit, the Bible, and other godly folks as our guides.

Now then, we are ambassadors for Christ, as though God were pleading through us: we implore you on Christ's behalf, be reconciled to God. (2 Corinthians 5:20 NKJV)

This means practicing real love to those who might have anger issues. And as we draw others to Him, God will do the rest. Remember, there is a reason they have come across your path and into your life. As spiritual diplomats, the fruit of the Holy Spirit is our job description to humbly serve others.

But the fruit of the Spirit is love, joy, peace, patience, kindness, goodness, faithfulness, gentleness, self-control; against such things there is no law. (Galatians 5:22–23 NASB)

CHAPTER 13

CALMING WORDS FOR THE SOUL

(Psalms)

God is our refuge and strength,
A very present help in trouble.
Therefore we will not fear...

(Psalm 46:1–2 NASB)

Biblical Background

The book of Psalms is a compilation of one hundred and fifty inspiring and uplifting hymns, songs, prayers, praises, and, at times, wise sayings. Like the book of Proverbs, these writings aim to provide insight into our relationship with God and others. Many Psalms reflect the human experience and resulting emotions, including anger, when going through all sorts of situations and circumstances spread across the full spectrum of life.

The Anger Solution

Generally speaking, most of us are grateful when life is "oh so sweet" and we are blessed and comfortable. We tend to thank God and exalt Him with praise in these times. We are also probably most agreeable to others, and we will often want to share our good cheer. On the other hand, life can sometimes be overwhelming and calamitous. When situations may not make sense or go the way we want them, we might become annoyed and even angry. Life can also bring much uncertainty, which can cause us to be troubled.

In these times, many of us might not praise God because we don't feel like it; we might not be so agreeable to be around. If that is the case, we might feel alone or even abandoned to the point of despair. But we can take comfort that the authors of the book of Psalms, including David, felt the same way. They cried out to God, especially when exhausted with what appeared to be nowhere to go.

> *Yea, though I walk through the valley of the shadow of death, I will fear no evil: for thou art with me; thy rod and thy staff they comfort me.* (Psalm 23:4 KJV)

So when things don't go our way, we can always pray to God, meditate on His Word, and praise Him! We can give our concerns to Him, even in the most challenging, troubling, or painful situations that cause us suffering, doubt, or anger. The book of Psalms reassures us that God is watching over us and is fully engaged in our lives. Therefore, Psalms can provide us the ability to:

1. Seek God's help (Psalm 18:6).
2. Receive God's comfort, safety, and rest (Psalm 4:8).
3. Have God's presence amid pain and suffering (Psalm 119:50).
4. Know that God's righteousness and justice will prevail (Psalm 37:39–40).
5. Trust God in all situations with His strength, blessings, and peace (Psalm 29:11).
6. Expect God to have a blessed plan for each of us (Psalm 20:4).

The psalmists fixed their eyes on God, taking the focus off themselves as the sole (or soul) problem-solver. May God richly bless you as you seek Him, His guiding hand, and His Word, whatever your situation might be in life. Like the psalmists, please focus not on the battle at hand but on God's victory to overcome that battle.

Points to Ponder

Seek God's justice, for He is righteous. Because He is righteous, God will administer His "due process" for lawbreakers who have no regard for truth or justice. Sadly, many of them are caught up in their own little worlds, not caring for others but loving only themselves. They believe they will get away with their immoral acts while hurting others along the way. Therefore, do not seek revenge for yourself or others. Instead, we need to trust God's justice and believe that He will do it rightly in His time!

If given the opportunity, consider yourself not as an adversary to others but as an ally. We can come alongside these people showing loving kindness and a willingness to offer a helping hand and speak to them in truth. By presenting the Gospel of Jesus it is possible to plant a seed and show them another way of life that includes a life full of blessings and not curses. Place them in the hands of a righteous God, knowing that justice will prevail in the end.

> *Righteousness and justice are the foundation of Your throne; Lovingkindness and truth go before You.* (Psalm 89:14 NASB)

Seek God's help by praying and waiting on the answer. These are the times when God desires to hear from us. Sometimes the answer might not be in our time, or it is not the precise answer we want. Still, God will answer our prayer in His time and in His way for His purpose. So continue to pray, and wait, no matter the circumstance. Please don't give up; be patient because God only wants the best for us.

Wait for the Lord; be strong and let your heart take courage; Yes, wait for the Lord. (Psalm 27:14 NASB)

Be a peacemaker at all times. Obviously, we will not get along with everybody in life, but that doesn't mean we shouldn't try. This can apply to anybody who comes into your life, be it a coworker, neighbor, family member, or whoever. It also means that, at times, you might have to be humble and swallow your pride to get along. God teaches us patience, humility, and kindness, allowing us to be genuinely concerned for others.

On the flip side, not everybody's going to like you, not everybody will respect you, and not everybody will care about you. Have you ever been on a team where folks didn't care about or respect each other? How did you feel? Did you find that it made being successful harder? Nevertheless, we can still try to get along with all others no matter the situation (at work, in the neighborhood, etc.) and be *peacemakers* and *peace-givers*, not *peace-takers*, for their sake as well as ours.

Depart from evil and do good; Seek peace and pursue it. (Psalm 34:14 NASB)

Remain calm if a situation heats up. When you find yourself in a confrontational situation with an argumentative person, do not make the situation worse by getting all hot and bothered. An excellent way to do this is by holding your tongue and controlling your body language. Undoubtedly, some people have the talent to spin others up, primarily for control reasons to see the response. For this reason, it is also essential to have identified your hot buttons and what might trigger you beforehand.

For instance, one trigger might be receiving criticism. There can be a fine line between advice (usually constructive and positive) and being attacked. We should remain calm and listen, especially if unsolicited "advice" is given. Sometimes, the instructive words can sound very sharp and hurtful. However, we might want to take an honest look at ourselves to see if the words have some truth. After all, if something needs to be corrected, that can be a good thing. If that is not the case, you may always choose to disregard the comments.

Similarly, if you are considering offering "helpful" advice to others, it is always wise to ask first if they are willing to receive it. Just as importantly, this includes proper timing. If a person is already upset, it is often wise to be patient and perhaps wait for a better time. If not, you may well find yourself in a "heated" situation and you might be the one having to cool it!

Refrain from anger and turn from wrath. (Psalm 37:8 NIV)

We are not alone in our pain and suffering. Each of us will face many trials in our lifetime. Some will be painful (i.e., a broken relationship, a job loss, a death of a loved one, etc.), and some will have us suffering (loss of health, etc.). Certainly, none of us is immune to adversity. However, we need not experience it alone. God will always be there. Many decide to feel sorry for themselves, throw a pity party, get angry, and see themselves as victims. But we can choose a more desirable path with God and together face difficulties head-on.

There is also reason and purpose in challenging moments when they come. Understanding that, we can truly be blessed by growing in character and learning to persevere in all sorts of conditions and hardships. In turn, we can come alongside others who are hurting or troubled because of what they are experiencing. Having gone through similar circumstances allows us to be genuinely empathetic and supportive.

When pain or suffering comes into our lives, we can choose what to do with it and who we share it with. Let God have it, because our strength is limited, and His is not. God will keep us, preserve us, and deliver us, no matter what we are going through.

But as for me, afflicted and in pain—may your salvation, God, protect me. (Psalm 69:29 NIV)

God will comfort us through life's journey. Life can sometimes be uncertain, especially when the situation may seem dismal, bleak, and depressing, even to the point of causing fear (as with Peter). Yet, as the Good Shepherd, God remains steadfast with His flock, watching over and caring for us. He is ever vigilant for any trouble ahead, continually leading and directing. If the path happens to be in a valley of darkness, God will get His loved ones safely through. The Good Shepherd's protection always surrounds us. With confidence in Him and not in ourselves, He will care for and comfort us in this journey, eventually getting us through.

> *Even though I walk through the darkest valley, I will fear no evil, for you are with me; your rod and your staff, they comfort me.* (Psalm 23:4 NIV)

Our hope is alive in God. Have you ever been in a place where you felt hopeless? If that is the case, pray about it, seek out God's Word, and meditate on it. While waiting for the answer, perhaps God desires you to learn patience and grow in faith. In this time, keep praising Him for who He is. Wait on God's response with an expectant heart and have hope in Him, looking forward to all He can and will do.

> *Be strong and let your heart take courage, All you who hope in the Lord.* (Psalm 31:24 NASB)

Do not worry! You have probably found that worrying is the opposite of trust. Time spent considering things that may or may not happen is time wasted. To a large extent, fretting can use a lot of energy with both mind and emotions actively engaged. A better course is often to act by praying, meditating on God's Word, and seeking godly counsel. Worry focuses on the problem. Faith in godly action concentrates on solving it. Which would you rather be doing?

Do not fret—it leads only to evil. (Psalm 37:8 NIV)

In God, we trust. God wants us to trust Him. God is there for us in all of life's situations, especially when it appears there might not be any other options. By stepping out in faith and placing our trust in Him, we allow God to take on whatever burden or trouble we have. Subsequently, we can step back and wait in joyful anticipation that God will do His best for us.

And those who know Your name will put their trust in You, For You, O Lord, have not forsaken those who seek You. (Psalm 9:10 NASB)

God has plans for your future. God desires only the best for you (Jeremiah 29:11). Hopefully, you have learned that God blesses you when you place your trust and faith in Him. Although life is a one-day-at-a-time undertaking, God is also looking to your future. He wants to hear from you, so tell him your desires. And with an eager heart, continue to praise God for all He has done and will do in your life. No doubt, the best is still yet to come!

For the Lord God is a sun and shield; the Lord bestows favor and honor; no good thing does he withhold from those whose walk is blameless. (Psalm 84:11 NIV)

May he give you the desire of your heart and make all your plans succeed. (Psalm 20:4 NIV)

CHAPTER 14

PEACEMAKING

(The Sermon on the Mount)

"Blessed are the peacemakers,
for they will be called children of God."

(Matthew 5:9 NIV)

Biblical Background

This "Sermon on the Mount" is found in both Matthew and Luke's Gospels and is most likely the same event. Jesus preached "new" concepts and ideas, creating the New Testament as He spoke. Matthew includes three large sections (chapters five to seven), while Luke's is much shorter (chapter six). They also differ in scope, with Matthew covering many more topics. Although both have an initial section on blessings, Luke includes "woes" (problems). For our purpose, we will address four critical areas preached by Jesus in both Gospels—peacemaking, anger, revenge, and loving others.

The Anger Solution

Peacemaking

> *Blessed are the pure in heart, for they will see God. Blessed are the peacemakers, for they shall be called children of God. Blessed are those who are persecuted because of righteousness, for theirs is the kingdom of heaven. Blessed are you when people insult you, persecute you and falsely say all kinds of evil against you because of me. Rejoice and be glad, because great is your reward in heaven, for in the same way they persecuted the prophets who were before you.* (Matthew 5:8–12 NIV)

The sermon begins with several attributes that all disciples of Jesus should possess. With each one comes a blessing. For example, if one mourns, one will be comforted, and if one shows mercy, that individual, in turn, will receive mercy. The blessings appear associated with one another. In other words, it is easier to be a peacemaker if one is already pure in heart, and it follows that if one possesses peace, one is in a better position when persecuted, insulted, or falsely accused. True peace comes from God (John 14:27) and is offered freely to all.

Yes, life can be complicated and filled with many problems, ordeals, and uncertainty. Perhaps you have gone through a very tough situation—for example, a medical procedure, a traffic accident, a disagreeable neighbor, a natural disaster, etc.—and yet, have received God's peace. Often, it can come about through prayer; peace is real because it comes from God (Philippians 4:6–7). If this peace is missing in your life, you will know it. It is part of what makes life harmonious. This peace gives our souls rest, removes our burdens and anxieties, and calms our troubled hearts, no matter what we face. No matter the circumstance, when we trust God, He will give us peace to get us through.

Many define peace as the state whereby they are without problems or conflict, and that is true to an extent. For others, it might mean living a "comfortable" life. But peace is more than both of these. One of the most important things to having peace in your life is to have a clear conscience and an honest and loving relationship with God and others. This means confession, asking for forgiveness, and doing the right thing, which can get rid of guilt, shame, etc. Unfortunately, many have become callous and behave accordingly, with much anger, resentment, bitterness, and little peace.

Peacemakers who sow in peace reap a harvest of righteousness. (James 3:18 NIV)

Anger

You have heard that it was said to the people long ago, "You shall not murder, and anyone who murders will be subject to judgment." But I tell you that

anyone who is angry with a brother or sister will be
subject to judgment . . . (Matthew 5:21–22 NIV)

These are some strong words. Of course, we know murder and anger are different. Murder takes another's life, while anger is usually an emotional display of displeasure or hostility. Anger can eventually lead to murder, but it typically ends up far short of any physical confrontation, with just a heated exchange of words. However, it appears that the two, murder and anger, are intertwined. Jesus states that anger will also get you judgment. He doesn't say a lesser judgment will be received if angry, but the same judgment as if one committed murder. Perhaps Jesus is saying this for a two-fold reason: (1) a deterrent not to get angry and (2) a reminder that anger can result in evil actions that can be highly unpredictable. Additionally, calling someone derogatory or contemptuous names is just as bad, particularly when angry.

Again, anyone who says to a brother or sister, "Raca,"
is answerable to the court. And anyone who says,
"You fool!" will be in danger of the fire of hell.
(Matthew 5:22 NIV)

Indeed, Jesus is saying that anger is a severe matter, so we ought to be careful how we treat and speak to others. Further, we should be cautious of name-calling, joking, making fun of, or ridiculing another person. Any one of these behaviors can push others' hot buttons and make them mad, resulting in unforeseen consequences. So please don't do it or participate in it. Be at peace with others.

> *Do not let any unwholesome talk come out of your mouths, but only what is helpful for building others up according to their needs, that it may benefit those who listen.* (Ephesians 4:29 NIV)

Revenge

> *You have heard that it was said, "An eye for eye, and a tooth for a tooth." But I say to you, do not resist an evil person; but whoever slaps you on the right cheek, turn the other to him also. If anyone wants to sue and take your shirt, let him have your coat also. Whoever forces you to go one mile, go with him two. Give to him who asks of you, and do not turn away from him who wants to borrow from you.* (Matthew 5:38–42 NASB)

Of all the passages in the Bible, the preceding is perhaps the most difficult that I have studied. Is it literal or figurative? For punishment in the Old Testament, the one who caused the injury would themselves pay with the same loss.

> *. . . life for life, eye for eye, tooth for tooth, hand for hand, foot for foot.* (Deuteronomy 19:21 NIV)

Going against this revenge and equal payment mandate, Jesus asks His listeners not to resist an evil person. He tells them not to seek personal payback for someone who might have caused the injury. Indeed, we don't go up against evil with evil; we go up against evil with good.

This passage seems to get progressively more challenging. We are to obey to the point of being slapped! If you have ever been struck on the head or face, it most likely hurt. Besides just physically, it possibly wounded your pride, especially if you were hit in front of others. Typically, if you don't defend yourself and stand prepared to strike back, the situation might escalate because if the offender can get away with a slap, they might try something more.

But it looks like Jesus is saying, yes, you got hit, but no, do not strike back. In fact, offer the other side of your face to the person as well. Well, that is a tall order for anyone. In obedience, let's say we turn the other cheek. Is Jesus literally saying that the best option is to be hit again and suffer, or is it figurative that the wisest choice is to offer a sign of peace? Or is it both? He also uses other examples of giving yourself to another to meet their needs, such as being sued, forced to do something against one's will, or lending.

Are all these things humanly doable? The answer is yes! But do we want to do them? That is the question. After all, each situation asks for self-control, restraint, and the desire to be at peace with others.

There is a cost to bear in each instance: offering them your cheek, your coat, your time, and your money. It might prove too costly. Given these, which will you choose to do? Please read on before answering.

> *Do not take revenge, my dear friends, but leave room for God's wrath, for it is written: "It is mine to avenge; I will repay," says the Lord.* (Romans 12:19 NIV)

Love for Enemies

> *You have heard that it was said, "Love your neighbor and hate your enemy." But I tell you, love your enemies and pray for those who persecute you, that you may be children of your Father in heaven.* (Matthew 5:43–45 NIV)

Love is an emotion; it also is a behavior that we can freely choose to exhibit with others. Jesus desires that we are loving individuals, placing others first, whether they are evil or not. So how does one love an enemy? Through actions. I submit that it is hard to get angry and remain angry with others you care about because you only want the best for them. However, when we don't care about others, it is easier to mistreat them, disrespect them, and, yes, get angry at them.

In final consideration, Jesus is saying we ought to treat that person we might not care about the same way we treat someone we love. Doing this minimizes the likelihood of having negative feelings for that individual. It could make all the difference in the world how you, in turn, are treated. To be sure, it can simply come down to viewing others as God does. For example, rather than seeing your neighbor as unlikable, a coworker as competition, and so on, consider liking them in brotherly or sisterly love. You might begin by saying a kind word or doing something nice for them. In time, hopefully, you will see a change in the relationship.

Points to Ponder

We are called to be at peace with ourselves and to make peace with others. If you're going to make peace with someone else, it helps first to be at peace with yourself, including your past. We shouldn't live in the past. We should live in the now and plan for the future. However, many people continue to live in the past with memories that hinder them from living a full life. Often, these thoughts are based on previous relationships that have gone sour. Past mistakes, regrets, hurtful actions, or anything else might still persistently weigh heavily in your thoughts. To help let go and forget, give them to God and move on with His Word, prayer, and forgiveness (including forgiving yourself), thereby receiving peace and healing (Psalm 34:17, 147:3; Jeremiah 17:14).

*But I will restore you to health and heal your wounds,'
declares the Lord,* (Jeremiah 30:17)

Forget the former things; do not dwell on the past.
(Isaiah 43:18)

*Brothers and sisters, I do not consider myself yet to
have taken hold of it. But one thing I do: Forgetting
what is behind and straining toward what is ahead,
I press on toward the goal to win the prize for which
God has called me heavenward in Christ Jesus.*
(Philippians 3:13-14 NIV)

*Therefore, if anyone is in Christ, the new cre-
ation has come: The old has gone, the new is here!*
(2 Corinthians 5:17)

When it comes to another person, the aim should
always be maintaining a peaceful relationship. Easier
said than done sometimes, as loss of peace often
begins with a disagreement; it can even be over a
simple misunderstanding. And with it can come
agitation, discord, and distress, ending in someone
being upset. If that is the situation, it can then escalate into a full-blown conflict. At this point, believers are called by God to de-escalate the situation.
The Bible would have us throttle back and maintain
self-control (Proverbs 16:32, 25:28; 2 Timothy 1:7;
2 Peter 1:5–7; Galatians 5:22–23; Titus 2:11–12). If
necessary, perhaps stepping away from each other
and pressing the pause button will help to restore
peace and the relationship.

Admittedly, not having a sense of peace can also affect many other things, including peace of mind, quality of sleep, stress level, and emotional or physical wellness. Living without peace can lead to making bad decisions, especially when restless, ill, agitated, troubled, or anxious. If you or someone you know is experiencing any of these, turn to God, pray, and ask Him to bless you with His peace:

1. To receive freedom from oppressive thoughts and emotions. (Galatians 5:1)
2. For rest. (Psalm 4:8)
3. For calmness within. (Psalm 29:11)
4. To be in harmony with others. (Colossians 3:13)

When we seek peace, we will be blessed. By obedience and love for God, His peace will benefit us as well as others.

They must turn from evil and do good; they must seek peace and pursue it. (1 Peter 3:11 NIV)

Truly turn the other cheek. As I have previously asked, what will you do if slapped? Would you turn the other cheek? On second look, perhaps a slap has an additional meaning.

Consider what a closefisted punch can do to the head if forceful enough. A blow landing on the side of the face might break cheekbones or cause eye damage, possibly permanently. If near the temple, it might even kill. A slap, on the other hand (no pun intended), is open-fisted and has flexibility. In other words, all the fingers will bend when they strike an object. The force is usually not enough to cause any significant injury. Still, temporary pain will undoubtedly ensue.

So what is a slap, and what is Jesus trying to teach us? It appears He is saying that a slap is merely an insult. And insults, you and I can handle. Why? Because as peacemakers, we are called to overlook insults. We are called to forgive and love, just as God has done with us. Perhaps, the next time someone insults you, smile and be kind. Hopefully, the person doing the insulting will think twice about continuing and wonder why you are not defending yourself or getting riled up. Therefore, will you please consider turning the other cheek? Again, it isn't only for our sake but for the other person; the focus is on them, not us.

> For if you forgive others for their transgressions, your heavenly Father will also forgive you. (Matthew 6:14 NASB)

> And so we know and rely on the love God has for us. God is love. Whoever lives in love lives in God, and God in them. (1 John 4:16 NIV)

CHAPTER 15

AGAPE LOVE

(1 Corinthians 13)

Love is patient, love is kind. It does not envy,
it does not boast, it is not proud. It does not dishonor others,
it is not self-seeking, it is not easily angered, it keeps
no record of wrongs. Love does not delight in evil
but rejoices with the truth. It always protects,
always trusts, always hopes, always perseveres.

(1 Corinthians 13:4–7 NIV)

Biblical Background

Love. If asked, what does this conjure up in your mind? For many, it could mean being "in love" with more of a romantic spin based on physical intimacy. Others might describe it as having a deep emotion or feeling. When non-romantic, love can be seen as a genuine affection for someone like-minded with a common interest or goal with whom we enjoy sharing. Another could define it as having a real fondness for a favorite *thing*. Additionally, love could mean having a fond memory of a situation or place or anything else one might deeply care about. Often, love is something we take delight in.

But what exactly is love? What does the Bible have to say about it? What is the connection between love, hate, and anger? And how can love impact us on how we treat others?

The Greek language has many words for love in the New Testament. One primary word used throughout is *agape*. Agape is beyond brotherly love; it is sacrificial love (John 3:16). It is more about how we should act and behave toward others (outside oneself) versus a feeling (inside oneself). Therefore, love is an act of the will to seek the best for others. This is how God treats us with His love because God is *agape* love (1 John 4:7–12).

The Anger Solution

Is this the type of love you practice? Do you genuinely care for others and their interests or needs? Do you look out for them, especially if you see a possible issue or problem they cannot see? The answer can get complicated because our feelings and emotions can also get involved and not let us see or act clearly. For instance, suppose you and another person are up for the same position at work; how much will you now care about them and their happiness? Does liking them or not liking them have an impact as well? Or perhaps you are at odds with someone close and reach an impasse; now what? As you can see, with feelings and emotions in the mix, how we behave can often be scenario- or relationship-driven, but should it be?

To be sure, the Christian answer is to love others with *agape* love. This type of love doesn't look at the situation or how you feel, but instead does what is suitable for the other person. Thankfully, we have a model to follow that Paul provided in 1 Corinthians Chapter Thirteen, famously known as the "love" chapter. Here, we find guidance in acting with and toward others for their best interest through *agape* love.

Paul knew this *agape* love to be true because of the dramatic turnaround in his life. He was known at first to be a hater. He was taught how to hate by Jesus's nemeses—the Pharisees. Then later, on the road to Damascus, he met Jesus. He was saved and transformed and began to preach the Good News. He demonstrated his love for God and others. Because Paul had lived and breathed hatred for much of his life, he knew the characteristics of hate (and later love).

What is the opposite of hate? It is love. And the opposite of love, therefore, is hate. Some believe that it is *indifference*. However, God's number one adversary, Satan, is far from being indifferent. He is a liar and a deceiver. Above all, Satan is a hater. He is in the business of actively destroying others with his many accusations and schemes of temptation (Revelation 12:10; 1 Peter 5:8; Matthew 4:1).

As an exercise, using the verses above in 1 Corinthians 13:4–7, let's substitute the word love with hate, showing the opposite characteristics of love (see below).

Hate is impatient, *hate* is unkind. *Hate* envies, *hate* boasts, *hate* is proud. *Hate* dishonors others, *hate* is self-seeking, *hate* is easily angered, *hate* keeps a record of wrongs. *Hate* delights in evil, but does not rejoice with the truth. *Hate* never protects, *hate* never trusts, *hate* never hopes, *hate* never perseveres.

Continuing the exercise, let's substitute the name Satan with hate, and we will discover that they are indeed interchangeable.

Satan is impatient, *Satan* is unkind. *Satan* envies, *Satan* boasts, *Satan* is proud. *Satan* dishonors others, *Satan* is self-seeking, *Satan* is easily angered, *Satan* keeps a record of wrongs. *Satan* delights in evil but does not rejoice with the truth. *Satan* never protects, *Satan* never trusts, *Satan* never hopes, *Satan* never perseveres.

Hate doesn't want to see the best for us, but the worst. Hate will do all it can to make life unbearable. It is self-centered and destructive (and often self-destructive). As an example, during Jesus's and

Paul's time, the religious leaders chose hatred over love. Theirs was a religion based on religiosity, not on a relationship with God. Although they believed they were very "moral" people, they did the opposite of loving others. Inside, they were dead spiritually. There was no genuine relationship with God. If there had been, they would never have treated Jesus the way they did.

> *Woe to you, teachers of the law and Pharisees, you hypocrites! You are like whitewashed tombs, which look beautiful on the outside but on the inside are full of the bones of the dead and everything unclean. In the same way, on the outside you appear to people as righteous but on the inside you are full of hypocrisy and wickedness.* (Matthew 23:27–28 NIV)

God asks us to act with love, not in the hypocritical way of the Pharisees. Thus, we should behave the same way He does toward us by loving others. Now, one step more, let's substitute the word God for love (for God is love), and we find:

God is patient, *God* is kind. *God* does not envy, *God* does not boast, *God* is not proud. *God* does not dishonor others, *God* is not self-seeking, *God* is not easily angered, *God* keeps no record of wrongs. *God* does not delight in evil but rejoices with the truth. *God* always protects, *God* always trusts, *God* always hopes, *God* always perseveres.

Next is a review of each verse of the "love" chapter. Please take your time, meditate, and study each characteristic of love, and truly consider if you struggle with any of them. If that is the case, prayerfully ask God to show you what hindrances or stumbling blocks there might be, and ask for help to overcome them. The goal is to incorporate these characteristics into your daily life to love God and others. Therefore, beginning with verse four:

Love is patient, love is kind. It does not envy, it does not boast, it is not proud. (1 Corinthians 13:4 NIV)

One of the main reasons people get angry is that they are NOT patient! Think about it for a moment. With patience, you have a time delay for cooling down. You can take a deep breath, step back, and pause to think. At this point, you can calmly size up the situation and consider possible alternatives. You don't need to be in a hurry to say or do anything, especially if you are on the verge of a potential conflict. Interestingly, patience is the first item on the list of characteristics of love, perhaps because it is that important.

Alongside patience is kindness. Kindness is often compassionate and can foster good feelings with others and self, especially when done in secret. Kindness through service to others can be appealing because it is an excellent and considerate way to treat others.

Next are envy, boasting, and pride—the antitheses of love. All three characteristics are self-centric and not others-centric. Truly, the religious leaders demonstrated all three. They were envious of Jesus's popularity, boastful of all the "religious" acts they did in public, and exceedingly full of pride—enough so that they couldn't admit any wrongdoing.

Jesus advises us to do the opposite and NOT be like them, for they were genuinely unloving folks. In practice, love can minimize or even prevent anger. It is much more difficult to get angry at others when you are a caring, respectful, compassionate, and loving person. And, in turn, it is more difficult for others to get mad at you when you are being genuinely loving and selfless.

> *It does not dishonor others, it is not self-seeking, it is not easily angered, it keeps no record of wrongs.* (1 Corinthians 13:5 NIV)

This verse is full of more *not* doing. When one disrespects and dishonors someone else, the offender often believes the targeted person or victim has little value or worth. Usually, this disrespect is meant to be done in a public forum with the chief aim to humiliate or embarrass. Any concern or consideration for the feelings of others is virtually nonexistent. Further, there is no sparing the hurt and pain inflicted, for it desires to damage. This uncivil action is often done out of anger, revenge, or unforgiveness, typically based on records of perceived wrongs. We are asked to do the opposite.

> *Love does not delight in evil but rejoices with the truth. It always protects, always trusts, always hopes, always perseveres.* (1 Corinthians 13:6–7 NIV)

When we practice respect, honor, and love of others, we promote peace, harmony, and healthy relationships. When we love, it is much easier to maintain self-control and not get angry. As a result of living these verses, one can rejoice with the truth and receive God's blessings of protection, trust, hope, and perseverance.

Now, one last exercise, let's substitute the word "I" for love.

I am patient, *I* am kind. *I* do not envy, *I* do not boast, *I* am not proud. *I* do not dishonor others, *I* am not self-seeking, *I* am not easily angered, *I* keep no record of wrongs. *I* do not delight in evil but rejoice with the truth. (With God) *I* will always be protected, *I* will always trust, *I* will always hope, *I* will always persevere.

Though it might seem to be a tall order to fill at first, and perhaps you might have found yourself lacking in some, all these characteristics are meant for us to live our lives in harmony with others. You might not get it right every time, and it will probably take some practice, but by living this way, you will begin to see its positive effect on yourself and others. This is undoubtedly the Golden Rule put into practice. And in doing so, you will become more and more Christ-like, following in His footsteps to show others *agape* love.

In conclusion, *agape* love desires only the best for others. Because we are God's children, we are called to love, honor, and respect Him and others. Being a Christian means being Christ's, and loving others as Jesus loves us. Yes, at times, this may seem hard to do, especially loving the very unlikable, the very despicable, the very (fill in the blank), but it is always possible to love with the help of the Holy Spirit. With Him coming alongside us to guide and support us, we can learn to get along with anyone, especially with those we feel are "impossible" to deal with.

> *We love because he first loved us. Whoever claims to love God yet hates a brother or sister is a liar. For whoever does not love their brother and sister, whom they have seen, cannot love God, whom they have not seen. And he has given us this command: Anyone who loves God must also love their brother and sister.* (1 John 4:19–21 NIV)

Points to Ponder

Love others by serving them. Serve rather than be served. This is a powerful way to demonstrate love for others. Jesus teaches that servanthood is a crucial characteristic of being a Christian. In His case, Jesus is both servant and king (Mark 10:45). Some leaders understand this and behave accordingly. They serve those they are serving and are thus beloved. However, this is not so for others desiring personal power and control.

Some people don't want to serve because they want to be served. They want to control the situation and other people, which can lead to misbehavior. If they don't get what they want, they just might get angry.

A case in point involves the religious leaders of Jesus's time. They were in authoritative and influential roles, but who among them cared about those they were supposed to serve? Clearly, weren't they serving their best interests by judging, influencing, and controlling others' behavior instead of loving God and others? To be sure, love was never part of it; power over the people was. The ruling class spoke smugly and proudly about what they did as if all were in the service and name of God. Instead, Jesus displayed (and offered) a direct contrast to them by what He said and did. Most noticeably, Jesus wouldn't conform to their traditions. When this happened, it made them angry.

No doubt, the religious leaders not only wanted Him to be like them but they wanted him to be placed under their thumb. Yet Jesus refused to be proud and a hypocrite, making them even angrier. In the end, these self-described followers of God showed much anger and hatred. It was certainly not the right way to show God's loving nature to others.

> *Woe to you, teachers of the law and Pharisees, you hypocrites! You clean the outside of the cup and dish, but inside they are full of greed and self-indulgence. Blind Pharisee! First clean the inside of the cup and dish, and then the outside also will be clean.* (Matthew 23:25–26 NIV)

The Pharisees lived a long time ago, but people like them with the same judgmental attitudes and behavior still exist. Just like the Pharisees treated Jesus, do not be surprised if you are treated the same way as a follower of Christ—even to the point of being hated, for some love to hate. A crucial question is: how do we get along with others (especially someone who doesn't like us and can push our buttons)? Simply put, love God first, and love others second.

> *"Love the Lord your God with all your heart and with all your soul and with all your mind and with all your strength." The second is this: "Love your neighbor as yourself." There is no commandment greater than these.* (Mark 12:30–31 NIV)

This will make us less apt to get irritated and angry. Is this doable for us today? Yes, because we are God's chosen people and called to do His will by loving others, always (Colossians 3:12).

Additionally, through God's love and the Holy Spirit, we can become more like Jesus, who served and loved, sacrificing His very life for us. Therefore, consider living a life full of sacrifice, humbly helping others, and being merciful and full of grace to those who doubt. Give of yourself, serve all and love all in Jesus's name.

Love others and forgive always. At times, we don't always say or do the right thing. If that happens, apologizing from the heart is undoubtedly the right thing to do. Saying sorry is always acceptable; however, sorry is a word that many of us rarely hear these days. It might be because of a reluctance to admit a mistake, the feeling that it might make one look weak, or not wanting to be held responsible. But sometimes, our conscience or the Holy Spirit will remind us of it until we take the appropriate action of apologizing.

Likewise, stubbornness can be at play when both parties are at fault, causing a stalemate because neither one wants to admit they are at fault. In which case, devoid of forgiveness, one or both parties will often become insensitive or indifferent to the other. This lack of sensitivity usually ends with keeping a record of wrongs, which can be stored away and later used for a possible heated encounter. Future meetings will invariably lead to words or deeds replete with anger, hate, and resentment.

Besides all of that, unforgiveness can discourage meaningful relationships with family members, friends, coworkers, or anyone else with whom you are close. If the underlying cause is not cleared up, a fracturing of the relationship may occur, with all communications ending. Unfortunately, some break-ups fare worse than others. For example, the result might be the silent treatment, a separation, or even divorce, and all because one or both parties refuse to communicate openly and honestly, they miss an opportunity to forgive the other. That being the case, a minor disagreement or misunderstanding can result in a full-blown disaster. Therefore, exercising *agape* love can often help resolve relationship issues and, at the same time, strengthen the relationship.

Many decades ago, I met a Christian couple and marveled at how well they got along and treated one another with respect, admiration, and kindness. They loved and were in love, genuinely caring for each other. When I asked what the one thing was for the basis of their success, the husband said it was the "last thing." Simply put, the last thing they did before they went to sleep would be to get on their knees and pray for each other. This allowed both to air things out in an open and honest forum before God and each other, to encourage and support one another, and show genuine caring. This was *agape* love in action. I didn't ask, but I suspect they prayed for each other throughout the day and would often say: "I love you."

I later thought to myself; it is hard to dislike somebody or be unforgiving when you're praying for them. One can feel a tremendous sense of peace in their soul if they are looking out for another's best interest without angst, doubt, or worry. This might be one of the best ways to resolve conflicts before they happen!

No doubt, it can sometimes be challenging to keep a relationship going. So be careful not to take one for granted. If you are on the verge of losing a relationship but are still on speaking terms, reach out to them to resolve any issues. If the connection is already broken, consider stepping out in faith and reopening communications. In both cases, the need for forgiveness might be at the heart of beginning the healing process. For this reason, show mercy and grace (and exercise a lot of patience) toward others, just like the Lord has done with you and me. It's okay to say, "I'm sorry." Try it. You might be pleasantly surprised!

Therefore, if you are offering your gift at the altar and there remember that your brother or sister has something against you, leave your gift there in front of the altar. First go and be reconciled to them; then come and offer your gift. (Matthew 5:23–24 NIV)

The Law, Jesus, and the Holy Spirit. The Law was made known to the Hebrews in the first five books of the Bible, but the religious leaders added more and more to it. Their "commands" gave them power and control, forcing obedience, which they reveled in. Those that broke the "law" received judgment and not forgiveness. Whereas Jesus came into this world to forgive. His very presence made the religious elite bitter and angry, seeking revenge on Him.

The major point is that we are no longer condemned under the law as the Pharisees were quick to do. Indeed, keeping the law doesn't save or provide for eternal life. Instead, when God sees us, He sees Jesus because of His sacrifice on the cross. Jesus became a substitutionary atonement for us and our sins. As a result, we are called to live a life that does not gratify our sinful nature. We are called to walk and be led by the Holy Spirit to live a life of holiness and love others.

Therefore no one will be declared righteous in God's sight by the works of the law; rather, through the law we become conscious of our sin. But now apart from the law the righteousness of God has been made known, to which the Law and the Prophets testify. This righteousness is given through faith in Jesus Christ to all who believe. (Romans 3:20−22 NIV)

Live by the Spirit and love by the Spirit. Live by the Holy Spirit and not by the way of the angry world. Being angry can be a lifestyle, and loving others can be a lifestyle. It is your choice which way to live. The Pharisees chose to live by the flesh and enjoyed a life that was contrary to the life Jesus lived. Today, those without the Holy Spirit live by ignoring God and pursuing all sorts of evil desires. Unfortunately, though there might be temporary pleasure, a life outside the Holy Spirit is never lasting or fulfilling (Galatians 5:19–21).

Of course, what is lasting is the pleasure and joy that comes from the Holy Spirit. With Him living inside us, the following is available to us now.

> *But the fruit of the Spirit is love, joy, peace, forbearance, kindness, goodness, faithfulness, gentleness and self-control. Against such things there is no law. Those who belong to Christ Jesus have crucified the flesh with its passions and desires. Since we live by the Spirit, let us keep in step with the Spirit. Let us not become conceited, provoking and envying each other.* (Galatians 5:22–26 NIV)

Thus, this is how we should live as Christians in an angry world: by doing God's will, maintaining a loving relationship with Him and others, and being led by the Holy Spirit. This allows us to treat others with tenderness, humility, tolerance, kindness, and forgiveness. That is genuinely living *agape* love!

> *Therefore, as the elect of God, holy and beloved, put on tender mercies, kindness, humility, meekness, longsuffering; bearing with one another, and forgiving one another, if anyone has a complaint against*

another; even as Christ forgave you, so you also must do. But above all these things put on love, which is the bond of perfection. And let the peace of God rule in your hearts, to which also you were called in one body; and be thankful. (Colossians 3:12–15 NKJV)

SECTION FOUR

NOW WHAT?

CHAPTER 16

YOUR HOT BUTTONS— NOW WHAT?

*Examine yourselves as to whether you are
in the faith. Test yourselves.*

(2 Corinthians 13:5 NKJV)

This is an excellent time to examine yourself and your spiritual growth. Because of the fast-paced world most of us live in, we don't have a lot of time to sit still and reflect on our lives, or even more to the point we may not want to, for fear of what we might find. But looking at oneself and one's actions, though it may be hard, shows maturity and the desire to improve. In that light, you might want to revisit the (hot button) scenarios in chapter two. However, this time, focus on what you *should* do, not what you *would* do. All those events listed took place before I wrote the book. Yes, knowing what I know now, I would have chosen differently in several of them, and perhaps you would too.

In chapter three, I mentioned that anger *usually* just doesn't happen spontaneously. Before someone "loses it," there's normally a buildup to that point. If one were to look back and think through how their anger might have started, it probably began with a minor irritant (from the same or a variety of sources). If the nuisance is not addressed and resolved, and other annoyances are added on, they will continue to build one on top of another without relief. It can reach a point where the person believes they have had it and can't take it anymore. They also might think they can no longer control themselves; therefore, they lose it and get angry. Undoubtedly, when that happens, they end up saying or doing something inappropriate. Without the ability to deal with irritants or annoyances, whether small or large, our buttons are ready to be pushed.

To aid us, we have looked at godly and ungodly people, their situations, and their hot buttons throughout this book. We saw how they responded when their buttons were pushed. It makes sense that we, too, recognize *what* makes us angry, *when* we are headed to or are at the tipping point, and *how* we respond (appropriately). So let's go through a couple of exercises.

Exercise 1. Let's figure out what your buttons are. They are anything that might bother, irritate, or annoy you. They can be a situation, issue, thing, etc. They become "hot" buttons if you reach the tipping point, go beyond it, and become angry, or it can also be some other emotion taken to its extreme.

The following is a list of possible buttons that may affect you. They include those from the hot button scenarios in chapter three, those in chapters four through ten, and others. Of course, this is not all-inclusive.

Abused	Avoided
Authority issues	Accident occurred
Bossed	Betrayed
Bullied	Broken trust occurred
Criticized	Corrected
Cheated	Control issues
Disrespected	Disappointed
Embarrassed	Fearful
Frustrated	Falsely accused
Gossiped about	Humiliated
Hungry	Ignored
Injustice	Insulted
Intolerant	Impatient
Impulsive	Interrupted
Looked down on	Lateness
Lied to	Losing something
Losing control	Mistreated
Morally outraged	Making a mistake
Medical ailments	Noise
Outrageous behavior	Physically hurt
Rejected	Threatened
Unprepared	Unforgiven
Waiting	

Do these look familiar? If so, I recommend you list them below and add any others you have identified. If you need more room, then write them on another piece of paper. THESE are your buttons. Write down as many as you would like, especially if they are reoccurring. Since buttons can change, you might want to revisit this section every so often.

My Hot Buttons:

Exercise 2. Like chapter two, let's write down some of your (hot button) scenarios and initial responses. You will need to:

1. Identify the situation.
2. Describe the feeling.
3. Decide if the reaction is God-centered or self-centered.
4. Put together an alternative godly response.
5. Identify your hot button(s).
6. Prepare a constructive solution that you may use in a similar situation.

It would look like this:

1. Situation: I am late for an appointment. I see what appears to be an open parking space. As I get closer and ready to pull in, I find another car has taken up two spaces. This means I must go around and keep looking as time ticks away.

2. Feelings: I feel frustrated because the other driver was rude by taking up two spaces. I must keep looking, waste more time, and probably be late.

3. Reaction: I became more agitated, hit my hands on the steering wheel. Although I finally found a spot, I was still late for the appointment and became hotter!

4. Alternative response: I could exercise patience, recite a Bible verse, and pray for an open parking space.

5. My button(s): being late, impatient, frustrated, and losing control (from Exercise 1 list).

6. Constructive solution (repeatable): Leave earlier, pray for traveling mercies, and have Bible verses ready.

Your turn. I recommend you use the following template and fill it out on another piece of paper. You can use this "scenario(s)" process repeatedly to work through hot button issues.

(Hot button) scenario(s)   **Date:**

My Situation:

My Feelings:

My Reaction:

Alternative Response (godly):

My Button(s):

My Constructive Solution:

Now, meditate and reflect on your hot button scenario(s). Did it get the results that you wanted? Did it help in the long run or make things worse? Were there unintended consequences? Was it a godly response? Suppose you found that the initial reaction was less than optimal, predominantly non-Christian. In that case, I recommend developing a Bible-based response that you might want to use in the future, especially if the situation is ongoing. Equally as important, if we are wrong or have wronged someone, we should admit it, accept the responsibility, and make the necessary amends. These actions can go a long way toward our spiritual growth.

Points to Ponder

Be prepared when your hot button is pushed! Indeed, before going into a situation that you have already identified as a hot button, the number one thing to do is prepare for it. As previously suggested, I recommend having one or two Bible verses set aside and ready to go. You can memorize or put them on small cards or your cell phone to be readily handy. Here are five relatively short examples:

Be kind and compassionate to one another, forgiving each other, just as in Christ God forgave you. (Ephesians 4:32 NIV)

And we know that in all things God works for the good of those who love him, who have been called according to his purpose. (Romans 8:28 NIV)

. . . bless those who curse you, pray for those who mistreat you. (Luke 6:28 NASB)

Set your minds on things above, not on earthly things. (Colossians 3:2 NIV)

But the fruit of the Spirit is love, joy, peace, forbearance, kindness, goodness, faithfulness, gentleness and self-control. (Galatians 5:22–23 NIV)

If that button is pushed and you become irritated or annoyed (and are tempted to become angry), try to remain calm, cool, and collected. Don't let your emotions control you; rather, exercise self-control and repeat the selected Bible verse(s) in your head. To be sure, *peace* is the goal. Yes, it might take some practice, but it is well worth it.

By the way, don't forget about your body language and how you communicate with others. As a helpful exercise, look in the mirror. Now, think angry thoughts and make some faces. That's what others see. Not so pleasant, right? Quickly, think of a Bible verse and relax, being at peace; what do you look like now? See the difference? Hopefully, there is one.

The look on their countenance witnesses against them . . . (Isaiah 3:9 NKJV)

The following are some more helpful tips that you might want to try. I pray you find the following attitudes, thoughts, and behaviors profitable. Perhaps try one a day over the next four weeks, as shown below, or choose any of the following (whether one or several) and concentrate on them throughout the day, making the world a less angry place with you in it.

Week 1

Sunday: Breathe and relax.

Monday: Think before you act.

Tuesday: Ask questions to clarify the situation or any misunderstanding.

Wednesday: Exercise your sense of humor and have a joke ready.

Thursday: Say something nice; give others a compliment.

Friday: Don't be confrontational.

Saturday: Be polite.

Week 2

Sunday: Meditate on a specific calming verse(s).

Monday: Be empathetic and put yourself in someone else's shoes.

Tuesday: Be prepared to forgive others; remember we forgive because God has forgiven us.

Wednesday: Smile.

Thursday: Encourage, don't discourage; build up, don't tear down.

Friday: Read key Bible verses on love and patience.

Saturday: Love with actions, not emotions.

Week 3

Sunday: Pray for others throughout the day and before going to sleep.

Monday: Be aware of body language, facial expressions, and gestures.

Tuesday: Pay for someone's coffee, snack, or lunch.

Wednesday: Notice people for something they have done well and mention it to them.

Thursday: Praise someone in public.

Friday: Say: "God bless you" when cursed.

Saturday: Be there and listen.

Week 4

Sunday: Listen to mellow Christian Contemporary music or Classical Instrumental Hymns.

Monday: Go out of your way and do random acts of kindness.

Tuesday: Read the book of Psalms while waiting in line.

Wednesday: Be at peace.

Thursday: Don't take revenge; let God handle it.

Friday: Share the gospel.

Saturday: In conversation, one can say: "I know how you feel. . . ." This doesn't mean you agree with what is said, but it acknowledges and respects the person.

Exercise 3. Now, add your own helpers here. (Remember to reflect on the following: living a godly life, showing love, exercising self-control, being others-centered, being respectful, and recognizing and acknowledging others' feelings). For further examples, they might look like this:

- Call, write, or email someone you haven't heard from in a while.
- Do a good turn for a neighbor.

- Memorize some calming verses.
- Let someone go ahead of you in line.
- Set aside a quiet time to read the Bible, meditate, and pray.

1.

2.

3.

4.

5.

6.

7.

8.

And forgive us our debts, as we also have forgiven our debtors. I am bringing up forgiveness again because it is THAT important in the "get angry or not" process. One of the biggest reasons people are angry is that they do not forgive, though God graciously forgives us. It is one of the keys to having a life of peace and being at peace with oneself. In other words, if we do not forgive others, regardless of the pain inflicted and the resultant suffering, not forgiving can further set in to cause resentment, anger, and finally, a desire for revenge in some form or another. All that "stuff" can cause one to be a prisoner of the past if not dealt with. Thus, we are called to forgive for our and the offender's good (a true win-win). In the same way, if the tables were turned and you offended someone (even unwittingly), and they refused to forgive you, how would you feel?

Clearly then, we should forgive, but why is it so difficult? The two biggest reasons may be 1) we want the other person to ask us for our forgiveness *first*, then we might consider forgiving them, or 2) we might want to have a debt that they owe us to hold over their heads. But these are not good reasons.

God is forthright; if we want Him to forgive us, we must forgive others *unconditionally*. This typically means we do the forgiving first. The sooner forgiveness is given and received, the sooner a broken relationship may be mended and restored.

On the other hand, if we don't forgive, unforgiveness can cripple us with all sorts of problems, including illness, emotional distress, grudges, ill will, and anger. If not resolved, misery will find a home to fester in an open wound over time. Recall the unforgiving servant earlier and what eventually happened to him (thrown in prison).

So one of the most significant ways to resolve anger is to be forgiving. Please don't hold on to anger and don't hold it in; forgive and forget! You can heal and be blessed with a greater probability of renewing any broken relationship. With that being said:

> *Be kind to one another, tender-hearted, forgiving each other, just as God in Christ also has forgiven you.* (Ephesians 4:32 NASB)

To be angry or not to be angry—a choice. No one is perfect, and given certain situations we might find ourselves in, we just might blow it. Therefore, we should always attempt to be polite and tolerant, even if others are not. Remember, getting angry is a choice based on free will. Recall Adam's decision: he had free will and made a horrible choice. As his descendants, we make choices every day; and sometimes, we don't make the right ones. These choices typically begin with a thought, followed by temptation, then become an act. Anger is no different. It's your choice to willingly give in to the idea of anger or take it captive and give it to God. So please choose wisely.

> *Trust in the Lord with all your heart, And lean not on your own understanding; In all your ways*

acknowledge Him, And He shall direct your paths.
(Proverbs 3:5−6 NKJV)

Anger and agape love. One of the biggest lessons I
have learned, and I pray that you have as well, is that
there is no need to get angry when you have *agape*
love. This type of love serves others. Because it is
predominately others-centered, it should preempt
any anger moment. I have attempted to practice all I
have written about, and if my hot button is pushed, I
do my best to let it go.

I now say: "Let go and let God!" Indeed, let the Holy
Spirit guide you in all matters. Continue to live your
life in *agape* love, for we are asked and called to do
that. Be a good servant and finish the race well. May
God bless you in your daily walk of faith to live a
godly life and help you keep your eyes on Him always.

*I have fought the good fight, I have finished the
course, I have kept the faith; in the future there is laid
up for me the crown of righteousness, which the Lord,
the righteous Judge, will award to me on that day;
and not only to me, but also to all who have loved His
appearing.* (2 Timothy 4:7−8 NASB)

CHAPTER 17

A FINAL POINT

*"Then the master called the servant in. 'You wicked servant,'
he said, 'I canceled all that debt of yours because
you begged me to. Shouldn't you have had mercy
on your fellow servant just as I had on you?' In anger
his master handed him over to the jailers to be tortured,
until he should pay back all he owed. 'This is how
my heavenly Father will treat each of you unless you
forgive your brother or sister from your heart.'"*

(Matthew 18:32–34 NIV)

Anger is part of living in a fallen world. Because of our current state, we can try to live the best possible lives by doing right by others and being at peace with all. If others don't act likewise, we can prayerfully show *agape* love, using the Bible as our standard for living and being led by the Holy Spirit. Thankfully, one day there will no longer be any anger for us, for we will be living in a place full of harmony and peace where all will get along—heaven. We should look forward to that day when we are in the presence of the holy and living God. However, if you are not a Christian, you might ask, how do I become one? I ask that you please consider the following.

Where will you spend eternity? In chapter nine, we looked at the parable of the wicked servant. In this story, Jesus wasn't only speaking about anger and forgiveness, but what happens to those who are without faith? Where will they spend eternity? Recall how the wicked servant is forgiven, but he cannot see beyond his vengeance. Rather than show mercy and grace to others, he then chokes his fellow servant. Because of his misdeeds, the wicked servant is tossed into prison. The prison in question is an allusion to hell. It is where people are sent after death, and it is eternal. By all accounts, it is a place of darkness and fire, full of torment (2 Peter 2:4; Mark 9:48; Matthew 13:50). It is a place no one should want to go.

But please take heart and read on.

The time is short. In truth, much of biblical prophecy has been fulfilled, and we are now in the end times.

The end of all things is near. Therefore be alert and of sober mind so that you may pray. (1 Peter 4:7 NIV)

The next event to occur is the rapture (Matthew 24:36–44). Jesus will descend and escort believers to heaven (John 14:1–4) because He is removing the church (His people) before the tribulation begins.

For the Lord himself will come down from heaven, with a loud command, with the voice of the archangel and with the trumpet call of God, and the dead in Christ will rise first. After that, we who are still alive and are left will be caught up together with them in the clouds to meet the Lord in the air. And so we will be with the Lord forever. (1 Thessalonians 4:16−17 NIV)

The tribulation is a seven-year period (Daniel 9:24−27), with great distress (Matthew 24:21) and many judgments of God to follow (Revelation 6:1−17, 8:1−12, 9:1−21, 11:15−19, 16:1−21).

Indeed, the time is short.

Jesus offers the gift of salvation. Time is fleeting, and hell is a place to be avoided at all costs. Thankfully, it is not too late for any of us, for we can be saved by faith. Most people can acknowledge some relationship with God and even call out to Him in times of need. However, there is *the* way to God, and it is through His Son, Jesus. Therefore, I encourage you to know the loving God through His Son, Jesus Christ.

Jesus answered, "I am the way and the truth and the life. No one comes to the Father except through me." (John 14:6 NIV)

When we accept the "Good News" message that Jesus is Lord and Savior, we have a promise that we will be saved and not perish in hell like the wicked servant.

Instead, our destination is heaven, with our eternal life guaranteed to be spent with God.

> *And I heard a loud voice from the throne saying, "Look! God's dwelling place is now among the people, and he will dwell with them. They will be his people, and God himself will be with them and be their God. 'He will wipe every tear from their eyes. There will be no more death' or mourning or crying or pain, for the old order of things has passed away."* (Revelation 21:3–4 NIV)

It is only by an act of faith that you and I are saved, and nothing more, for Jesus does the saving, not us. It is a gift freely offered to be willingly accepted, for Jesus is that gift. Hopefully and prayerfully, if that is the desire of your heart today, you can do this by simply affirming the verses below:

> *For God so loved the world that he gave his one and only Son, that whoever believes in him shall not perish but have eternal life. For God did not send his Son into the world to condemn the world, but to save the world through him.* (John 3:16–17 NIV)

> *. . . that if you confess with your mouth the Lord Jesus and believe in your heart that God has raised Him from the dead, you will be saved; for with the heart a person believes, resulting in righteousness, and with the mouth he confesses, resulting in salvation.* (Romans 10:9-10 NASB)

And by saying this simple prayer:

Heavenly Father, I believe that Jesus died on the cross for my sins. I repent of my sins. I accept Jesus as Lord and Savior. I may rejoice in the knowledge that if I died today, I would be in the presence of you, God. Thank you, God, for being a loving and forgiving holy God. Amen.

Last:

> *"The Lord bless you and keep you; the Lord make his face shine on you and be gracious to you; the Lord turn his face toward you and give you peace;* (Numbers 6:24-26 NIV)

POINTS TO PONDER (BY CHAPTER)

Chapter Four: Cain and Rejection

Beware of Satan's wiles.

Anger is part of our sinful nature.

When tempted to become angry, there is always a way out.

It is wiser to ignore a slight.

Anger blocks out rational thinking and reasonable conduct.

Pride goes before disgrace.

When angry, it is all right to reach out and share with others how you feel.

Anger can reflect a lack of faith and trust.

Anger can lead to further abuse and violence.

Anger can lead to disobeying authority.

Consider how your actions today will affect your future.

Chapter Five: Moses and Personal (In) Justice

Anger can often cause quick responses.

Taking justice into your own hands, whether justified or not, has consequences.

Managing anger may be a lifetime effort.

God can allow good to come out of a bad situation.

Chapter Six: Saul and Disobedience

Anger (with disobedience) can often limit our spiritual life.

Anger (with disobedience) leaves no peace.

Anger (with disobedience) is often tied to trust issues.

Anger (and foolishness) can make for bad decisions, so pray!

Chapter Seven: Haman's Revenge

Anger can lead to wicked schemes, plots, and plans.

Anger and hatred can lead to one's downfall.

God protects His own against angry and hate-filled people, especially those who would do evil.

Chapter Eight: A Servant's Unforgiveness

Anger can consume!

God's anger is just and forgiving!

Forgive and let go!

Forgiveness and unforgiveness have consequences.

Forgiveness is hard sometimes!
Practice forgiveness DAILY.

Chapter Nine: An Older Brother's Resentment

Be careful in judging others!
It is always better to overlook an offense.

Chapter Ten: Peter Acting Rashly

Do not repay evil with evil!
Practice self-control in all situations.
Put your fear in the right place.
Trust God in all things.

Chapter Eleven: Paul and Hatred's Blindness

Hate can destroy your life.
Be careful who you follow.
When you come to a fork in the road, choose wisely.
Having relationships means loving others.

Chapter Twelve: Choosing Wisely (Proverbs)

A fool's way leads to many problems.
A hot-tempered person can end up in all kinds
of trouble.
Wickedness and anger often go hand in hand.
Poor choices can lead to anger and harmful
consequences.
Avoid quarrels; they only lead to strife!

Be patient and stay calm!
Exercise diplomacy!

Chapter Thirteen: Calming Words for the Soul (Psalms)

Seek God's justice, for He is righteous.
Seek God's help by praying and waiting on the answer.
Be a peacemaker at all times.
Remain calm if a situation heats up.
We are not alone in our pain and suffering.
God will comfort us through life's journey.
Our hope is alive in God.
Do not worry!
In God, we trust.
God has plans for your future.

Chapter Fourteen: Peacemaking (The Sermon on the Mount)

We are called to be at peace with ourselves and to make peace with others.
Truly turn the other cheek.

Chapter Fifteen: Agape Love

Love others by serving them.
Love others and forgive always.
The Law, Jesus, and the Holy Spirit.
Live by the Spirit and love by the Spirit.

Chapter Sixteen: Your Hot Buttons

Be prepared when your hot button is pushed!

And forgive us our debts, as we also have forgiven our debtors.

To be angry or not to be angry—a choice.

Anger and agape love.

Chapter Seventeen: A Final Point

Where will you spend eternity?

The time is short.

Jesus offers the gift of salvation.

ABOUT THE AUTHOR

Robert Selekman has faithfully served the LORD in various capacities as a Preacher/Teacher, Deacon, Ordained Minister, Police Chaplain, Missionary Pastor, Christian Grief Counselor, and Christian writer. He is the author of *Touched by God's Tears: A Biblical Perspective on Death, Grieving, and Hope.*

Reverend Selekman became a Christian through the Navigators Ministry as a young Naval Officer. He subsequently made it a career, serving worldwide, including in the Gulf War, and retiring with the rank of Commander.

He eventually attended seminary and later became an ordained Minister. He possesses five college degrees, including an MBA, MA in National Security and Strategic Studies, and M Divinity. After traveling the world, he now lives in Southern California, serving the local church and volunteering with public safety. He enjoys writing non-fiction, counseling, and photography.